STUDENT UNIT GUIDE

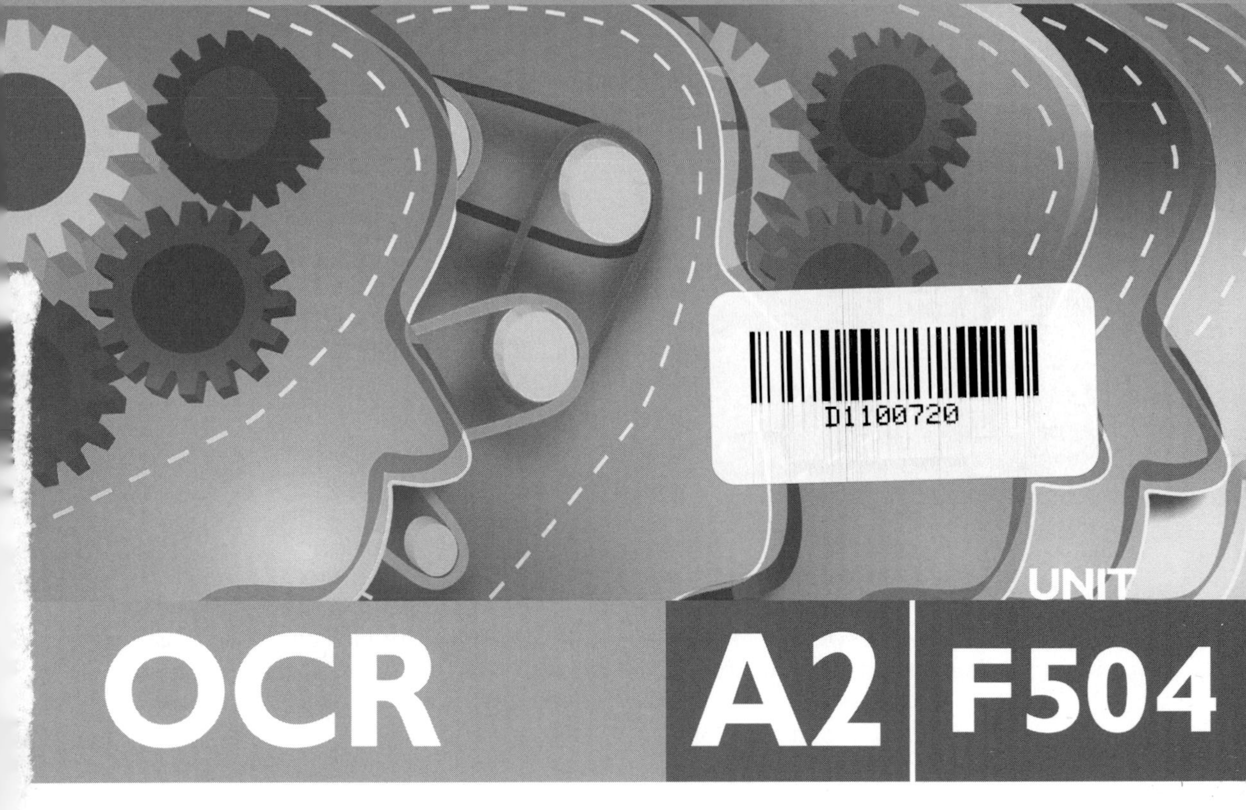

UNIT

OCR A2 F504

Critical Thinking

Critical Reasoning

David Yates

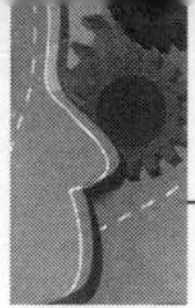

For Poppy

Grateful thanks to Roy van den Brink-Budgen, Jenny Bignold, and the critical thinking students at New Hall School, Chelmsford and St John Payne Catholic Comprehensive School, Chelmsford

Philip Allan Updates, an imprint of Hodder Education, an Hachette UK company, Market Place, Deddington, Oxfordshire, OX15 0SE

Orders

Bookpoint Ltd, 130 Milton Park, Abingdon, Oxfordshire, OX14 4SB
tel: 01235 827720
fax: 01235 400454
e-mail: uk.orders@bookpoint.co.uk
Lines are open 9.00 a.m.–5.00 p.m., Monday to Saturday, with a 24-hour message answering service. You can also order through the Philip Allan Updates website: www.philipallan.co.uk

ISBN 978-1-84489-556-4

First printed 2009
Impression number 5 4 3 2 1
Year 2014 2013 2012 2011 2010 2009

Typeset by Phoenix Photosetting, Chatham, Kent
Printed by MPG Books, Bodmin

P01439

Contents

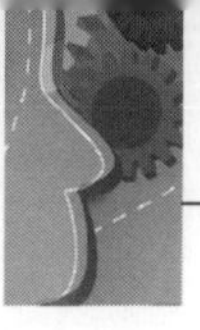

Questions and Answers

Introduction

About this guide

This guide is written for students following the OCR A2 Critical Thinking course. It deals with Unit F504 (Unit 4): Critical Reasoning.

It is not intended to be a comprehensive and detailed set of notes; you will need to supplement this material with further reading.

The guide is divided into three sections:

- This **Introduction** provides an outline of the demands of the unit, the format of the exam paper and the skills required to complete the unit successfully. There is also some general guidance on preparing for the examination.
- The **Content Guidance** section introduces the key skills required for Unit F504 and provides important advice on how to tackle the three sections of the exam paper.
- The **Questions and Answers** section includes four passages that reflect the complexity required for this unit. There are sample examination questions on each passage, and model answers on the first three. Sample A-grade and C-grade responses, together with commentaries, are provided for the questions on the fourth passage.

Unit F504

This is the last of the four units in the OCR A-level in critical thinking. None of the skills examined in this unit should be entirely new to you, as you will be taking this unit at the end of the course and it is intended to be a synoptic assessment. This means that, rather than being introduced to new skills, you should be developing your existing skills of:

- analysing arguments
- evaluating arguments
- developing reasoning of your own

The exam passages in Unit F504 will be longer and more complex than you have previously encountered, and the flaws will be less obvious and the structure less clear. Your own reasoning should be more developed.

In AS Units F501 and F502, you were directed to part of a passage and asked to comment on it. In Unit F504, you will be directed to a paragraph or several paragraphs, and you will be expected to take an overview of the content and to make several points of assessment.

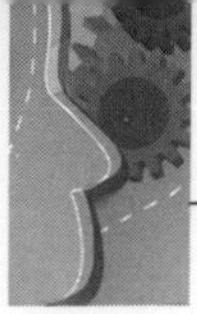

Resource booklet

The resource booklet will contain at least one passage, which will normally be quite a long article of the sort that appears in the comment and analysis pages of quality newspapers such as *The Times*, the *Daily Telegraph*, the *Guardian* and the *Independent*. Passages could alternatively be taken from journals, books or magazines.

It is possible that you may also be presented with other data, such as images, statistics and/or diagrams.

Skills

Critical thinking is different from other subjects because there is little subject content. Instead of expecting candidates to repeat learned facts, the focus is on the development and assessment of skills. In this unit, the key skills required are described below.

Analysing structure

You must be able to identify the elements in an author's reasoning, such as reasons, conclusions and intermediate conclusions, counter-arguments, examples and evidence.

Evaluating the reasoning

You will be expected to evaluate the reasoning of the author. This means being able to comment on the strengths and weaknesses in the overall argument. Key questions to ask include:

- How successfully has the author supported his or her conclusion?
- Can I identify flaws in the reasoning?
- How effective are the examples, evidence and analogies?
- Does the argument rely on assumptions? If so, are these assumptions reasonable?
- Have counter-arguments been dismissed successfully?
- Is the author's reasoning consistent?

Developing your own argument

At AS, your own arguments were expected to be short but carefully structured. In Unit F504, you are expected to produce one developed argument. Although this argument will be longer than those at AS, to be successful it will also need to be carefully structured. It should be clear, logical and persuasive. It is likely to include:

- several strands of developed reasoning
- well-chosen examples and evidence that support the reasons
- intermediate conclusions
- developed counter-arguments

Preparing for the examination

Practising skills

Unlike in most other subjects, in critical thinking no revision is really necessary. There are, however, several things that you could usefully do to prepare for your examination, and all of these include practising your skills.

First and foremost, the skills developed in critical thinking are supposed to be transferable to other subjects and to life generally. Good critical thinkers are likely to:

- want to be inquisitive and well-informed
- enjoy reasoned debate
- trust in the process of reasoned inquiry
- be open minded (avoiding bias or prejudice)
- understand the opinions of others (without necessarily agreeing with them)
- be willing to reconsider their own views where honest reflection persuades them that their initial judgement may have been mistaken

A weak critical thinker would be likely to agree with statements such as:

'I prefer jobs where the supervisor says exactly what to do and exactly how to do it.'

'No matter how complex the problem, you can bet there will be a simple solution.'

'I don't waste time looking things up.'

'I hate when teachers discuss problems instead of just giving the answers.'

'If my belief is truly sincere, evidence to the contrary is irrelevant.'

'Selling an idea is like selling cars, you say whatever works.'

Source: Facione, P. A. (1998) *Critical Thinking: What it is and why it counts*

Not everyone enjoys thinking critically. For some people, the subject takes them out of their 'comfort zone' because they have to face controversial issues and they may associate argument with disharmony. However, argument is not the same as quarrelling. People engaged in an argument are not necessarily falling out with each other on a personal level. Argument is an intellectual process that should involve a search for the truth.

In most A-level subjects, you will find that simple repetition of learned facts will not guarantee a good grade. Increasingly, examiners are expecting you to *analyse* and *evaluate* and to form judgements of your own. Your critical thinking skills should help you succeed at these higher-level thinking tasks.

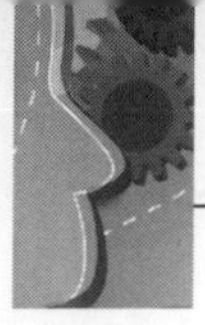

Reading articles

One of the most important things you can do to prepare for this examination is to get used to reading long articles from quality newspapers. The major broadsheet newspapers, such as *The Times*, the *Daily Telegraph*, the *Guardian* and the *Independent*, all have 'comment and analysis' pages every day, which contain articles, essays and arguments from some of the UK's leading commentators. These articles are available, free of charge, on the newspapers' websites.

The more of these articles you read, the easier it will become. You will develop in your ability to identify where argument exists within a longer article and to follow the reasoning of the authors.

Listening to arguments

Listening to the arguments of others is also good preparation for this examination, and beneficial to your A-level studies in general. Programmes such as the *Today* programme, *Any Questions?* and the *Moral Maze* on Radio 4 are highly recommended and you can listen for free, and at any time, on the BBC's iPlayer.

Further reading and viewing

Books

Whyte, J. (2003) *Bad Thoughts*, Corvo

Entertainingly exposes many examples of sloppy thought.

Levitt and Dubner (2005) *Freakonomics*, Allen Lane

'A rogue economist explores the hidden side of everything.' The authors seek to explain why drug dealers still live with their mothers, what teachers have in common with sumo wrestlers and why the legalisation of abortion may have cut the crime rate.

Baggini, J. (2008) *The Duck that Won the Lottery*, Granta

A hundred short 'thought experiments' relating to bad arguments.

Films

Capturing the Friedmans (2003)

A family is torn apart by child abuse allegations as they capture the sorry saga on home-movie cameras to create a compelling documentary. Were they wrongly convicted?

Thank You for Smoking (2005)

A smooth-talking spokesman for the tobacco industry tries to defend the indefensible. Can he convince you?

Bowling for Columbine (2002)

Michael Moore's most critically acclaimed movie, exploring American gun culture, is based around a 1999 massacre at a high school in Colorado. What conclusions can reliably be drawn from Moore's presentation of evidence?

Who Killed the Electric Car? (2006)

How many weaknesses can you find in this conspiracy theory?

My Kid Could Paint That (2007)

Marla, aged four, is declared a child prodigy and her paintings sell for over $25,000, until the family is 'exposed' as fraudulent by a television news report. The documentary explores the credibility of these allegations and it also considers the meaning and value of 'art'.

The examination

The examination lasts for 90 minutes, and you must answer *all* the questions on the paper. It is marked out of 60, and comprises 25% of the total A-level marks.

Many candidates worry about running out of time, and therefore want to start writing straight away. However, you should spend sufficient time reading and digesting the passage(s) in the resource booklet before putting pen to paper. Read the whole passage at least twice, and think carefully about what the author is trying to argue and how he or she has gone about it.

Apart from Question 1, there are no short questions. Each question is worth between 10 and 20 marks, so answers should be well developed. All questions relate to the resource booklet, which will contain one or more passages.

Because of the lack of subject content, there is no need to stay up late revising the night before the examination; have a good night's sleep instead.

There are three sections on the paper:

- **Analyse** — identify the structure of the passage
- **Evaluate** — assess the reasoning of the author
- **Develop your own reasoning** — write up your own argument

The total marks for each section add up to 20, so each should be regarded as equally important in terms of the allocation of time. A sensible time allocation for this examination would be:

- Studying the resource booklet — 15 minutes
- Analysis questions — 25 minutes
- Evaluation questions — 25 minutes
- Your argument — 25 minutes

Content Guidance

As Unit F504 is intended to be a synoptic unit, none of the skills involved should be entirely new to you, nor should it be necessary to introduce them as if they are new.

Instead, this Content Guidance section focuses on how the skills introduced at AS can be developed and applied to the new level of challenge presented by F504.

The three chapters relate to the three sections of the examination paper, which are:

- analysing structure
- evaluating reasoning
- developing your own reasoning

Each chapter includes revision of key skills and concepts and guidance on tackling the sample papers.

Analysing arguments

Structure of arguments

The first section of the paper (analysis) asks you to identify the structure of an author's argument.

Not everything in the passage will be argument. In some passages, large sections are devoted to what has been called 'scene-setting' material, in which the author is describing or explaining the background to the issue, as opposed to developing an argument.

The questions on the paper will direct you to parts of the passage that do contain argument, and you will be asked to identify how this argument has been constructed. It is important to remember that you are not being asked to evaluate the author's reasoning or to develop arguments of your own. If you disagree strongly with the author, this can be tempting, but do try to resist such temptation because you will have ample opportunity to evaluate and to argue in the later questions.

There will be two types of question in this first section:

- In the first type of question, you will be presented with a single sentence or part of a sentence. You will be asked to identify and briefly explain the function of this element in the structure of the author's reasoning. With these questions, there will usually be 2 marks available. The first is for successfully identifying the element and the second is for explaining its function in the argument.
- The second type of question will direct you to a whole paragraph and ask you to 'analyse in detail the structure of the reasoning'. For this type of question, you need to rewrite the whole paragraph, identifying each element as you go.

To tackle these questions, you need to be aware of the different elements that can be found in arguments and the function performed by each. These are shown in the following table.

Elements of an argument

Element	Function
Conclusion	The main conclusion brings an argument to a close and will be supported by much of the reasoning found elsewhere in the argument.
Reason	A reason supports a claim and may be backed up by evidence or examples. Reasons may work together (joined reasons) to support the conclusion, or they may work independently.
Intermediate conclusion	An intermediate conclusion supports the main conclusion. It is supported by reasoning found elsewhere in the passage.
Example	An example will be intended to support a reason. If you identify an example, say what it is an example of.

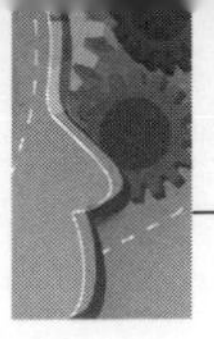

Element	Function
Evidence	Evidence will be intended to support a claim. If you identify evidence, say what claim it is intended to support.
Counter-argument/ counter-assertion	The difference between a counter-argument and a counter-assertion is in the presence of reasons. An argument must contain a conclusion and at least one reason. In longer passages, counter-arguments can be quite developed, with intermediate conclusions, examples and evidence of their own.
Response to counter-argument	Following a counter-argument, you can expect the author to offer a response. This should be identified as a response to the counter-argument. Evidence and examples can be included in this response.
Assumption	An assumption is unstated. It is something that the author must believe, in order to make his or her argument. An assumption is a missing link in the reasoning. Because an assumption is unstated, it would be a mistake to quote a sentence from the passage and then identify it as an assumption.
Analogy	A reason may be presented in the form of analogy. This is where an author compares two things. There is an implication that because *x* is like *y*, then it follows that the two things being compared (*x* and *y*) should be treated in the same way.
Hypothetical reasoning	A reason may be presented in the form of hypothetical reasoning. This is the 'if…then…' style of reasoning (see also p. 18). For example: '*If* you work hard and revise thoroughly, *then* you will probably pass your exam.' In this example, the author's conclusion that you will probably pass your exam is dependent on a condition that you must work hard and revise thoroughly. The author does not know if you will work hard and revise thoroughly but is prepared to venture that, *if* you do, *then* you will probably pass.

Abbreviations and diagrams

The following abbreviations are sometimes used by the examiners:

R = Reason

C = Conclusion

IC = Intermediate conclusion

Ex = Example

Ev = Evidence

CA = Counter-argument

A = Assumption

HR = Hypothetical reasoning

Ag = Analogy

You may use your own abbreviations; you may also use diagrams to illustrate the structure of arguments. If you choose to use abbreviations and/or diagrams, you *must* provide the examiner with a key to show what your symbols and abbreviations mean.

The specification makes it clear that diagrams are not essential, nor are they acceptable on their own.

Worked example

Some people have argued that the use of CCTV cameras should be limited because innocent people are filmed as they go about their lawful business and because CCTV evidence contributes to only 3% of criminal convictions. However, this 3% represents thousands of criminals who would have got away with their crimes, were it not for CCTV. The privacy campaigners did not complain when the perpetrators of the 7 July 2005 London bombing were caught thanks to CCTV evidence. This and many other cases show that dangerous people have been caught and convicted thanks to evidence from CCTV cameras. We should think more about the rights of the victims than the privacy of the criminals. Ordinary, law-abiding people should not be worried about being filmed by CCTV, if they have nothing to hide. Far from limiting the use of CCTV, we ought to be expanding its use.

The paragraph starts with a counter-argument. The conclusion of the counter-argument is that the use of CCTV should be limited, and this conclusion is supported by two reasons: that innocent people are filmed and the evidence that CCTV only contributes to 3% of criminal convictions.

The author responds to the counter-argument with a reason: that the 3% represents thousands of criminals who would otherwise have got away with their crimes.

The author then offers the example of the London bombers who were caught thanks to CCTV evidence.

The intermediate conclusion is that many dangerous people have been convicted as a result of evidence from CCTV cameras.

A further reason is that the rights of victims of crime should take precedence over the rights of criminals.

The final reason is that ordinary law-abiding people should not be worried about being filmed by CCTV cameras *if* they have nothing to hide. This is an example of hypothetical reasoning, since the author's assertion that people have nothing to fear applies only *if* it is true that they have nothing to hide. Some ordinary law-abiding people may have something to hide, even though they are not engaged in criminal activity.

This final reason relies on an unstated assumption that there is little chance of law-abiding people being wrongly convicted as a result of CCTV evidence.

The main conclusion of this passage is that we ought to be expanding the use of CCTV instead of limiting it.

The structure of this argument, therefore, is:

CA: Some people have argued that the use of CCTV cameras should be limited because innocent people are filmed as they go about their lawful business and because CCTV evidence contributes to only 3% of criminal convictions.

In the counter-argument, there are two reasons working independently to support the conclusion.

R1: However, this 3% represents thousands of criminals who would have got away with their crimes, were it not for CCTV.

Ex: The privacy campaigners did not complain when the perpetrators of the 7 July 2005 London bombings were caught thanks to CCTV evidence.

IC: This and many other cases show that dangerous people have been caught and convicted thanks to evidence from CCTV cameras.

R2: We should think more about the rights of the victims than the privacy of the criminals.

R3: Ordinary, law-abiding people should not be worried about being filmed by CCTV, if they have nothing to hide.

HR: This reason (R3) is an example of hypothetical reasoning. People may have something to hide, even if they are ordinary and law-abiding.

A: There is an unstated assumption that there is little chance of innocent people being wrongly convicted by CCTV evidence. The author must believe this; otherwise he or she would not be able to conclude that innocent people have nothing to fear from CCTV.

C: Far from limiting the use of CCTV, we ought to be expanding its use.

Evaluating arguments

When you evaluate the reasoning of an author, you are coming to a judgement as to how successful the author has been in supporting his or her claims.

You are looking for strengths as well as weaknesses in the reasoning. The articles in the resource booklet will be real passages written by learned people and it is unlikely that they will make no sense at all. If you think that an intermediate conclusion has been well supported by the reasons, that an example has been well chosen or that an analogy is effective, then say so.

There will be some flaws, irrelevant appeals, misused statistics and/or inconsistency but, overall, how problematic are these? Just because an author has been guilty of some technical errors, it does not necessarily follow that the overall argument has completely failed. It may be, for example, that the argument has fallen short of complete success but some of the claims may be well supported.

Remember that few arguments are completely logical in the formal sense. In longer passages, the best the author can usually hope for is to persuade the reader that his or her conclusion is *probably* true.

A major error made by some candidates in answering the questions in this section of the paper (evaluation) is that they launch into counter-argument. Such candidates are so incensed by the author's point of view that they start to develop an argument of their own to counter the author. Although tempting, this is not what the examiners are looking for. You need to concentrate on evaluating the reasoning of the author rather than developing an argument of your own.

Validity of arguments

The modern study of argumentation owes a great deal to the philosophers of ancient Greece, such as Socrates, Plato, Aristotle and the Sophists.

Many people in ancient Greece found that they needed to argue a case in court, and they turned to the Sophists to teach them the skills of **rhetoric** (the art of using language to persuade) to help them present their case effectively. In ancient Greece, and later in Roman society, the ability to speak persuasively in public was an important skill.

Even today we recognise the importance of rhetoric and we still teach presentation skills and the art of public speaking. However, we are also rightly suspicious of those whose skills of rhetoric are so good that they can actually persuade an audience to accept bad ideas. This was exactly the criticism of the Sophists 2,500 years ago: that they could be helping their clients to persuade an audience that the weaker case was actually the stronger. Effective speakers and writers can persuade people to accept illogical arguments by means of rhetorical tricks such as appealing to emotion or prejudice.

For the Sophists, the aim of an argument was to win it, which is still the objective of the modern debating team. The problem is that the truth surely *does* matter and we do not want people to be persuasive unless their case is logical. This is why Aristotle developed a system of **formal logic**.

Syllogism

For Aristotle, the most perfect form of argument was the *valid* syllogism. In a syllogism, there are two reasons (usually called 'premises') followed by a conclusion. In a valid syllogism, if the reasons are true, then the conclusion follows with certainty. Consider this example:

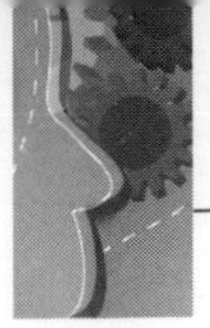

Premise 1: All teachers drink coffee.

Premise 2: My father is a teacher.

Conclusion: Therefore, my father drinks coffee.

This argument is deductively valid because, if the two reasons are true, then the conclusion must logically follow.

The example also illustrates one of the limitations of formal logic, which is that an argument can be deductively valid even if the reasons are false. It is not true that all teachers drink coffee, nor is it true that my father is a teacher. The argument is entirely counterfactual, yet it is still a deductively valid syllogism.

This type of logic allows **hypothetical reasoning**, in which we can show that the conclusion must be true *if* the reasons are true. Through hypothetical syllogisms, the 'if ... then ...' style of reasoning was developed, as in this example:

If Jake is the murderer *then* the gun will be in his house.

The gun is not in Jake's house.

Therefore, Jake is not the murderer.

This argument is deductively valid, but again it is unsatisfactory in other ways. The problem is not with the logic of the syllogism but with the reliability of the supposition (the hypothesis) that *if* Jake is the murderer *then* the gun will be in his house. Jake may have hidden the gun elsewhere.

Syllogisms become invalid only when the conclusion does not follow from the reasons, and this is where the first formal flaws were identified. Consider this example:

All dogs have four legs.

My cat has four legs.

Therefore, my dog is a cat.

This argument is invalid. Even if the reasons are true, the conclusion would not follow with certainty. Even if all dogs do have four legs, it does not logically follow that everything with four legs is a dog.

Deductive syllogisms can be useful in presenting the formal logic of an argument. However, they also have limitations: most of the arguments we use in everyday life cannot easily be reduced to syllogistic form, and the truth of the reasons generally does matter.

Inductive reasoning

Formal logic is a specialised type of reasoning; most of the argumentation in which we engage most of the time is **inductive**.

In a strong inductive argument, the conclusion will *probably* be true, even though it cannot be said that it is certainly true. Here is an example of a strong inductive argument:

> Jake confessed to the murder. The murder weapon was found in Jake's house. Jake's fingerprints were on the gun. Jake's DNA was found at the murder scene. Jake had a strong motive to commit the murder. Therefore, Jake must be the murderer.

Even if all the reasons are true, we cannot say with 100% certainty that Jake is the murderer. However, it would be reasonable to conclude that Jake is *almost certainly* guilty.

However, not all inductive arguments are as convincing. Here is a final example:

> Jake had a motive to commit the murder. Jake cannot provide an alibi for his whereabouts at the time of the murder. Therefore, Jake must be the murderer.

We can see that the induction in this example is much weaker. Although Jake could be guilty, he should probably not be convicted on this evidence alone.

The arguments you will encounter in F504 will use mainly inductive reasoning. You need to consider how strongly the reasons support the conclusion. It is also necessary to spot logical errors that may be present in the reasoning. We call these 'flaws' and they are considered below.

Flaws

A flaw is a common but erroneous pattern of reasoning that weakens an argument. It represents an error in logic.

At AS, you should have learned the names of some of the most common flaws. The following table may be useful as a reference.

Name	Description	Example
Ad hominem	Attacking the arguer rather than the argument. A personal attack is not, in itself, a flaw. What matters is how relevant the personal attack is to the argument being made.	George W. Bush claims that it was a good idea to invade Iraq, but we know that he hears voices in his head that he interprets as being instructions from God. Therefore, the invasion of Iraq was a bad idea.

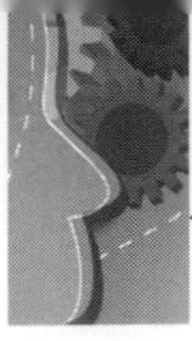

Name	Description	Example
Tu quoque	Arguing that two wrongs make a right.	'My doctor told me to lose some weight but why should I listen to a doctor who is himself overweight?'
Post hoc	Arguing that *x* happened and then *y* happened. Therefore, *x* must have caused *y*.	'I went to a different newsagent to buy my lottery ticket and I won £1,000. I am definitely going to buy my lottery tickets from that shop in future.'
False cause	Similar to post hoc in that it relates to causation. False cause could describe any argument where the author suggests that correlation must equal causation. Just because there is a link between two things, it does not follow that one thing must have caused the other.	'People who smoke cannabis have a higher prevalence of psychiatric disorders compared to those who do not. Therefore, smoking cannabis causes mental illness.'
Conflation	Using different words, terms or ideas as if they mean the same thing.	'We know that growing your own vegetables has become much less popular in recent years because there has been a sharp decline in the number of allotment holders.'
Restricting the options (false choice)	Arguing that there is a straight choice between two options, when there may be other options.	'Either you accept that I saw an alien spacecraft or you must think I am a liar.'
Confusing necessary and sufficient conditions	Just because doing *x* is necessary to achieve *y*, it does not automatically follow that doing *x* will be sufficient to achieve *y*.	'I have all the qualifications for this job and all the required experience. I made my application by the deadline and I have good references. Therefore, I will definitely get the job.'
Hasty generalisation	Generalising from a limited sample or from a single example.	'That school is a bad school. I know someone who went there and she said that the teachers were horrible, the other pupils bullied her and she failed all her exams.'
Sweeping generalisation	Failing to accept that, with most generalisations, there are sensible exceptions that can be made.	'It is well known that girls do well at GCSE. Therefore, although Vicky Pollard is an inarticulate and unmotivated single mother, who once swapped her baby for a Westlife CD, she is bound to do well in her exams.'

Name	Description	Example
Circular argument (begging the question)	An argument that goes round in circles, so that the conclusion is a repetition of the reasons.	'You know that I am a good person for this job because my friend has given me a glowing reference. You know that my friend is a reliable person because I can vouch for his character.'
Straw man	Distorting the argument of an opponent and then attacking the distorted version rather than the real argument.	'The government says that the school budget has to be cut by 5%, so it obviously doesn't think it is important that children should learn to read and write.'
Slippery slope	An argument that goes too far too quickly; suggesting that, if one measure is taken, a whole chain of events will follow.	'If we allow gay people to marry people of the same sex, then we would have to legalise polygamy, and then we would not be able to stop people marrying children or animals.'

Emotional and irrelevant appeals

Rhetorical appeals can help to win a debate, but they often weaken the reasoning because they seek to sway an audience with emotional persuasion instead of rational argument.

These appeals are flawed only if they are *irrelevant* to the argument. For example, appeals to authority can be extremely relevant as good evidence. An appeal to authority is irrelevant if it is to someone who is not an authority in that field.

Another example would be the appeal to popularity. In a democracy, popular opinion is often important evidence for deciding what ought to be done; the flaw occurs when someone argues that what the majority thinks must necessarily be correct.

At AS, you should have learned the names of some of the most common rhetorical appeals. The following table may be useful as a reference.

Name	Description	Example
Appeal to emotion	Authors may appeal to emotions, such as fear (scaremongering) or pity (a sob story).	'You can't give me a bad grade for this work because I tried really hard and it took me ages to do.'
Appeal to authority	Appealing to an authority that is not an authority in that field.	'Chelmsford is not worth visiting. Charles Dickens despised Chelmsford, describing it as "the dullest and most stupid spot on the face of the Earth".'

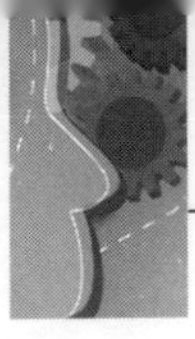

Name	Description	Example
Appeal to popularity	Appealing to popular opinion in cases where popular opinion is not relevant. Just because the majority of people think something, it does not necessarily follow that they are right.	'The majority of people think that attacking Iraq was a bad idea. Therefore, attacking Iraq was a bad idea.'
Appeal to history	Arguing that what has happened in the past will happen in the future. Evidence of past performance cannot necessarily predict future performance.	'The stock market has crashed but it is bound to bounce back because this is what has always happened in the past.'
Appeal to tradition	Confusing *is* and *ought* If something has been done for a long time, it does not automatically follow that the practice is sensible.	'These rules have been established for many years. Therefore, we should not change the rules.'

Analogies

If the passage in the resource booklet contains an analogy, this is certainly an opportunity for evaluation.

You will remember from Unit F502 that an analogy is a comparison between one thing and another, for the purposes of argument. A good analogy can strengthen an argument, but a poor analogy will weaken it.

It is important to be precise about exactly what the author is comparing. Take the following as an example:

> 'Children are tested too much at school. You don't fatten a pig by weighing it all the time.'

A weak candidate might simply say that the author is claiming that schoolchildren are like pigs.

A stronger candidate would understand that the comparison is between testing a child and weighing a pig only insofar as both processes are intended to measure the extent to which progress is being made towards meeting an objective. The author is making the point that *excessive* testing of children uses up curriculum time that could be better spent teaching new things, just as weighing a pig takes time that could be better spent feeding it.

This is quite a strong analogy, helping to make the point that the more testing takes place (especially in modular GCSEs and A-levels), the less time teachers have to deliver the curriculum.

Assumptions

In F502, you should have learned that an assumption is an *unstated* reason in an argument.

An assumption is something that the author has not said, but nevertheless must rely on in order to make the argument. It can be said to be a 'missing step' in the reasoning.

Here is an example of an argument that relies on an unstated assumption:

> There have been two film versions of Roald Dahl's *Charlie and the Chocolate Factory*. The 2005 version, starring Johnny Depp as Willy Wonka, is the better movie because it is more faithful to the plot of the original book.

The assumption is that a movie adaptation of a book should be faithful to the original story. The author has not explicitly stated this, but it must be something that he or she believes to be true in order to draw this conclusion.

This assumption is not necessarily a weakness in the argument. That would depend on whether or not the assumption is *reasonable*. Would anyone want to question the assumption?

Many people would disagree with the assumption that a movie adaptation of a book should be faithful to the original story, but this author has offered no reasons to support a contentious view. It would, therefore, be reasonable to say that the author's argument is weakened because of a lack of reasoning to support this missing step in the argument.

Evidence

Evidence may be offered in an attempt to strengthen an argument. It may take the form of percentages, averages, rates or raw numbers. In the examination, it is not necessary to question the accuracy of these figures, since you would not be able to verify the data in those circumstances. For the sake of the evaluation, you can take it that the author has not just made up the evidence.

Even if the figures are correct, however, you do need to approach the evidence critically. At AS, you should have encountered numerical data and learned to question the reliability of such data.

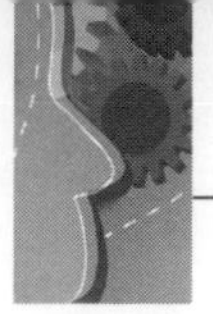

If an author offers statistical evidence as part of an argument, the most important question to ask is whether or not this evidence supports the conclusion. Is the evidence supporting the point that the author is trying to make?

There follows two examples of how the use of statistical evidence can be evaluated.

Opinion polls

Poll or survey evidence is commonplace, and there may be an opportunity to question the reliability of such figures.

Polling companies like to regard their work as a science, and it is remarkable how accurate their sampling can be. By questioning fewer than 800 people, a poll can accurately reflect public opinion in a population of 60 million, so beware of making a comment such as, 'The poll cannot be trusted because it didn't ask everyone'. With opinion polls, the quality of the sample (whether it is a representative selection of genders, ages, income groups etc.) is more important than the sample size.

Irrespective of how many people are questioned, a poll taken of randomly selected people in a town centre on a weekday afternoon is unlikely to be reliable; the same could be said of polls of self-selecting samples, such as phone-in, write-in or website polls.

It is important to consider carefully the questions that were asked and the conclusions that could be safely drawn. A poll asking people if they are concerned about knife crime does not necessarily indicate support for greater police powers to stop and search. If people say that they are generally supportive of initiatives to encourage recycling, it does not necessarily follow that they would be supportive of less frequent rubbish collections.

You also need to consider the extent to which public opinion is relevant to the argument. In a democracy, we value the will of the electorate but it does not necessarily follow that the majority view will be the right view. Public opinion is frequently inconsistent and it can change rapidly.

A-level results

There is an annual controversy over A-level results. More than 25% of A-level results are now at grade A and, overall, results have risen every year since the early 1980s. From this evidence, some conclude that the exams have become easier, while others claim that it is proof that the government's educational reforms have had a positive effect on the quality of teaching and learning. Thus the same evidence can support opposing conclusions.

The argument of the government, that rising results are evidence of the success of their education policies, is post hoc, because there are many other possible reasons why A-level results have increased, and it is even possible that the results have increased *in spite of*, rather than *because of*, government policies.

The evidence of rising results is also insufficient to support the conclusion that the exams must have become easier. Maybe young people are achieving better results because they are more intelligent or more motivated compared to students some 25 years ago. A further problem is that the A-levels of today are very different to those taken in the early 1980s, especially since the introduction of coursework, of the AS and of unlimited retakes of modules. Because the qualification has undergone many changes, comparing an A-level of today with one of so many years ago is not comparing like with like.

Examples

Examples are a type of evidence intended to support generalisations. In evaluating the usefulness of examples, you need to ask two questions:

- Have a reasonable number of examples been offered?
- How relevant are the examples?

Recently it has been claimed that many young people are studying 'soft options' at A-level, and one example that is often cited is media studies. On its own, an example of a single subject would not be sufficient to support the claim that many young people are studying soft subjects. This would be a hasty generalisation, in which the author has *generalised* from a single example or an insufficient sample.

A further problem arises because it is not universally agreed that media studies is, in fact, a soft subject. Therefore, the *relevance* of the example could be questioned.

If an author has offered several examples in support of a claim, each example needs to be considered in turn. If one example is weak, because of questionable relevance, the author loses the example, but the extent to which this damages the overall argument will depend on the number and relevance of the other examples and evidence.

Consistency and inconsistency

Authors may weaken their arguments by contradicting themselves, or there may be more subtle inconsistency, for example through shifting definitions.

Contradiction and inconsistency certainly weaken an argument but they are not necessarily fatal. If there is a contradiction or an inconsistency, it means that the author cannot be right in both cases. The author may lose part of the argument but not necessarily all of it.

Counter-arguments

The difference between a **counterclaim** and a **counter-argument** is that a counter-argument will include reasons in support of the alternative conclusion. A counterclaim

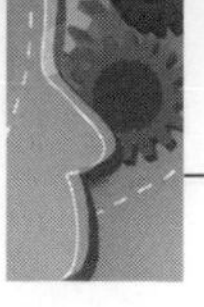

will just acknowledge that there is an opposing point of view, while a counter-argument will be more developed.

Weaker candidates sometimes make the mistake of interpreting a counter-argument as contradiction. Such candidates are misinterpreting the intention behind the counter-argument, which is to outline the opposing point of view before dismissing it.

A good counter-argument can strengthen an argument because it shows that the author understands and has considered the opposing point of view. However, the author does need to *dismiss* the counter-argument effectively, otherwise the counter-argument may appear stronger than the author's own case.

Causation

The flaws table on pp. 19–21 reminds you of the problems with post hoc and false cause. These flaws are so common that they merit some more attention.

Let us start with an example of a post hoc argument:

> They put a speed camera in our village. Since the camera was installed, there hasn't been a single fatal accident. Therefore, speed cameras save lives.

The argument is post hoc because the reasoning is that A happened and then B happened, so A must have caused B. The flaw is that B may have happened anyway. In this case, the speed camera is not necessarily preventing fatal accidents. It would be interesting to know how long the speed camera had been present and what the fatal accident rate was in this village before its installation.

Post hoc arguments are also used by people who oppose speed cameras:

> Since they installed a speed camera, the accident rate has increased. Therefore, it is clear that speed cameras cause accidents.

The problem here is that we do not know what the accident rate would be without the speed camera. It is possible that the speed camera is preventing some accidents and that it is not causing the accidents which do occur.

Remember that *correlation does not prove causation*. If there is a connection between two things (A and B), then it is often concluded that A caused B — but this is not the only possibility. In fact there are four possibilities:

- A did cause B.
- B actually caused A (reverse causation).
- The connection between A and B is a coincidence.
- A and B were caused by a third factor.

Here is an example:

> A study of men in Hungary has found that men who carry mobile phones in their back pockets have lower sperm counts.

From this evidence, we could conclude that A caused B, that carrying a mobile phone in the back pocket causes a lower sperm count (maybe because of the radiation from the phone).

With this example, few people would conclude that B caused A. The idea that having a low sperm count causes a man to carry a mobile phone in his back pocket is unconvincing.

A coincidence is also unlikely, particularly if the researchers conducted a wide study and found a strong correlation between carrying a mobile phone in the back pocket and having a low sperm count.

However, we cannot be sure of the conclusion that the radiation from the mobile phones is damaging male fertility: further investigation is needed. We need to search for alternative explanations (a possible third factor).

One explanation could be that Hungarian men who carry mobile phones in their back pockets tend to be smokers. They use their breast pocket for their cigarettes and the low sperm count could, therefore, be caused by smoking.

Overall strength of the reasons

Having focused on factors such as examples, evidence, assumptions and analogies, it is useful to take a general overview of the strength of the author's argument. You need to consider the extent to which the reasons support the conclusion.

It is probable that the argument will have strengths and weaknesses; you should acknowledge both.

The chances are that one flaw, one bad example or one minor inconsistency will not, on its own, invalidate the whole argument. Where weaknesses exist, you need to consider the extent of the damage to the overall argument.

Developing your own arguments

In F502, you were asked to develop two or more short arguments of your own in response to the reasoning of the author. In F504, you will be asked to write a longer, more developed argument.

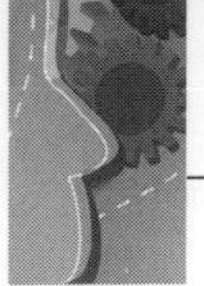

Many candidates manage to write three or four pages, but it is important to remember that the examiners are seeking to reward the *quality of the reasoning* rather than the length of the response. It is better to write a shorter argument that is carefully planned than a long passage of rambling waffle.

The examiners strongly recommend that you spend 5 or 10 minutes thinking about and planning your argument. Think about the reasons you will use, the order in which you will present these reasons, and the evidence and examples that you will use to support your claims.

The examiners will be looking for certain elements to award marks. They want to see:

- three or four strong reasons
- evidence and examples
- key words clearly defined
- a use of intermediate conclusions and counter-argument

However, the examiners are also assessing the overall quality of the reasoning; a carefully structured argument is more likely to be logical, coherent and convincing than one that has been less well planned.

Conclusion

Your argument should contain a clear main conclusion. This conclusion needs to be accurate, as directed by the question on the paper.

Definitions

At the start of the argument, you need to consider the extent to which key words or terms might be vague or ambiguous. You then need to define these terms by stating precisely what you will take these words to mean for the purpose of your argument.

Reasons

You should be aiming to develop about three strong and distinct strands of reasoning to support your main conclusion.

Examples and evidence

You should aim to include *strong* evidence and examples that support your reasons.

You are not expected to have precise facts and figures at your fingertips during the examination, but nor is there usually any need to invent evidence. The chances are that you will know something about the issue under consideration and that some facts and examples will occur to you during your planning.

Some candidates may be tempted to make up opinion poll figures or a quote from an invented 'expert' because these are easy things to throw into an argument. However, this may represent a weak appeal to popularity or authority. If '73% of people in a poll' supported a particular course of action, what does this actually prove? If 'Professor X of Y university' is quoted, is the expertise of this authority relevant?

The important thing is that evidence is used well to support your reasoning. You need to think carefully about the link between the 'fact' and the reason it is intended to support.

Intermediate conclusions

Each strand of reasoning will include a statement of the reason and, ideally, some expansion in the form of supporting evidence or examples. Having explained the reason, you should aim to draw an intermediate conclusion before proceeding to the next strand of reasoning.

An intermediate conclusion may simply summarise or repeat the reasoning in the paragraph. This would be a weak intermediate conclusion but it would be better than nothing. It would at least show some structure in the argument.

A stronger intermediate conclusion would be one that moves the argument forward in some way, providing a link to the next line of reasoning. This is one advantage of thinking about the order in which you will present the reasons in your argument.

Counter-arguments

The presence of a counter-argument in your reasoning will show you understand that there is an alternative point of view. The purpose of including a counter-argument, however, is not to show that you are fair minded and balanced. You are not supposed to be sitting on the fence.

The real purpose of presenting a counter-argument is to dismiss it. Therefore, including a counter-argument is a good idea but only if you can provide a strong reason why it should *not* be accepted.

Things to avoid

You should by now be well aware of the things that weaken arguments, such as unreasonable assumptions, logical flaws, emotional appeals and inconsistency. Clearly, it is a good idea to avoid such errors in your own argument.

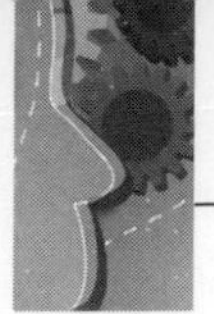

The best way to minimise such flaws is to *plan* and to *think*. Under exam conditions, candidates are often stressed and worried about running out of time, and in this panicked state they often concentrate on writing as much as possible in the hope that at least some of the content will gain credit. On this question, however, this is not a good strategy, because the examiners are looking for structure, logic and consistency. Remember that your argument is much more likely to have such qualities if you take the time to plan a structure.

Questions & Answers

This section contains four sample resource booklets (Samples A–D), with typical examination questions on each.

On the paper in the examination, it can be expected that there will be three sections:

- **Analyse:** This section will probably be worth 20 marks. You can expect that the questions will ask you to identify the function of certain elements in the passage in the resource booklet and you may also be asked to analyse in detail the structure of a paragraph. In this guide, Samples A, B and C include both types of analysis question. Sample D includes only questions on identifying the function of elements.
- **Evaluate:** This section will probably be worth 20 marks. You can expect to be asked to evaluate the reasoning of the author in parts of the passage in the resource booklet. You may also be expected to evaluate the reasoning of authors responding to the original article. In this guide, Samples A and D include both types of evaluation question. Samples B and C include only questions on evaluating the reasoning in the original article.
- **Develop your own reasoning:** You can expect one question, worth 20 marks. In this guide, Sample D includes a typical question.

The questions in Samples A–D are accompanied by model A-grade answers. Sample D also includes some poorer responses, which may be C-grade answers, with examiner's commentaries (indicated by the symbol e) on how the answers could be improved. There is some examiner's guidance (also indicated by the symbol e) on how to tackle Question 5 in Sample D, developing your own argument.

Sample A

Resource booklet

If I could choose, I'd have far less choice in my life

Treating children as little consumers is wrong

I grew up with precious little choice about anything. You ate what you were given, 1
went to school where you were told, wore your sister's hand-me-downs (sometimes, to be honest, ate some pretty second-hand stuff too). And twice a year —
birthday, Christmas — you got a present.

We weren't poor at all but that was entirely normal and I don't remember feeling 2
remotely deprived. Today, as we can see all around us, children seem to have
everything — designer clothes, computer games, fussy eating habits and the attention span of itchy gnats. A report yesterday from the Children's Society found that
one in ten kids now has mental illness diagnosed and it concluded that materialistic consumer pressure may be partly to blame, with children from poor backgrounds the main victims.

Where is it coming from, this consumer pressure? First, from television, and the 3
false dreams on offer there (we didn't watch much telly either).

Children from poor backgrounds, as well as having less money to buy the latest 4
clothes or electronic games, are more likely to have parents without time to spend
with them, and homes without access to outside space, so are far more likely to
end up spending hours in front of the telly soaking up adverts alongside the easy
gratification offered by cartoon, fantasy or drama.

You cannot just blame the parents for this; many will be working hard, with no 5
choice, just to put food on the table (some will be cleaning your house or looking
after your children); after all, how many can afford a house with a garden in a city
or suburb these days? On the *Today* programme yesterday, the chief executive of
the Advertising Association, Baroness Buscombe, argued that advertising to children could be a social good, among other things contributing to healthier lifestyles.
I profoundly disagree, I think it is overwhelmingly damaging. It exists to sell things
— toys, dreams, promises. That's all.

Of course parents can correct bouts of consumerism in their children by teaching 6
them what is and is not affordable, but why subject them to the clever traps of marketing people in the first place? Pressure is bad enough as it is, from schoolfriends
and celebrity excess, without allowing some of the cleverest adult minds in the
sharpest advertising agencies in the world to manipulate them as well.

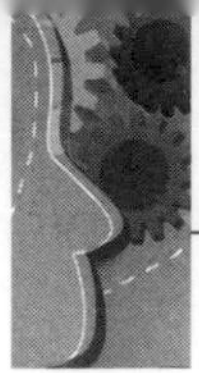

'We want to turn this on its head in a sense and talk about how we can empower parents and children,' Lady Buscombe added. 'I mean, have they asked parents, do they want children's programmes, because of course commercial broadcasters rely on advertising to fund children's programmes.' Well, do we want commercial children's television? Couldn't we live without it? Her comment betrayed an interesting assumption: that children have a right as consumers to as wide a choice of programmes as possible. 7

But why is it in a child's interests to be treated like a consumer? It has yet to be proven that giving even adults a wide range of choices improves their lives. In many instances, from too many yoghurts in the supermarket all the way up to a supposed choice of doctor or school, it is just confusing and stressful. I think the fewer, carefully selected, choices we can give young children, the more we help them. Watch the exhausted face of a six-year-old confronted by all this year's Christmas presents, without the time to play with any of them for more than a few minutes, and see what I mean. 8

But choice is the buzzword of the moment, and we are all supposed to be in favour of it, even when, as in choice of school for instance, it translates into that panicking six-year-old, now a worried 11, being made to pay for the gap between a political rhetoric of choice and the reality of a stressed-out parent obsessing over league tables. 9

What are we teaching here? What is everyone, from the politician who parrots choice in public services to parents squeezing their children through tortuous entrance criteria to Lady Buscombe, teaching those kids? That they have a right to a wide choice, in everything. It isn't true. There is no automatic right. 10

And so these disappointed little consumers, already angry and isolated, fed on a diet of socially alienating television and straitjacketed testing regimes, grow up to hang morosely around shopping centres (watching the adults consume). There, we as a society routinely allow, even actively encourage, their literal social expulsion. 11

The Archbishop of Canterbury, Rowan Williams, yesterday joined the campaign against the Mosquito, the high-pitched machine, unbearable to teenage ears, which sends them fleeing from shops and arcades. It is hard to conceive of a more antisocial way of dealing with groups of mooching adolescents with nowhere to hang out; it is astonishing that we accepted the introduction of this offensive machine into a supposedly civilised society without a murmur. In other spheres, wouldn't we call it torture, or at least some form of bodily harm? Having buzzed them off with Mosquitos, we have the pleasure of watching angry, isolated teenagers morph into depressed adults who demand Prozac from the doctor — because I've got a choice, haven't I? It's my right: I don't have to take some exercise if I don't fancy it. I choose the little pill. 12

The hundreds of millions of pounds spent by the NHS on prescriptions for antidepressants that may after all have been largely ineffectual is one of the prices of the consumer society, where I get what I want. 13

(Incidentally, did it strike anybody else that the idea of 'publication bias', where drug companies withhold inconvenient results about the efficacy of a drug they want the NHS to prescribe, is more commonly known as 'lying' or even 'fraud'?) 14

We are spoilt, and we are spoiling our children. They need to be taught to look down as well as up; to choose to feel fortunate, and not envious — and to recognise that gratification isn't as easy as buying a new toy or switching on a dream. And, as my mother would have been delighted to hear, it will not cost a thing. 15

Source: Alice Miles © *The Times*/NI Syndication (27 February 2008)

Analysis questions

Identify and briefly explain the function of the following elements in the structure of this argument:

(a) 'A report yesterday from the Children's Society found that one in ten kids now has mental illness diagnosed...' (paragraph 2) (2 marks)

(b) 'On the *Today* programme yesterday, the chief executive of the Advertising Association, Baroness Buscombe, argued that advertising to children could be a social good, among other things contributing to healthier lifestyles.' (paragraph 5) (2 marks)

(c) 'We are spoilt, and we are spoiling our children.' (final paragraph) (2 marks)

■ ■ ■

Model answers

(a) This is evidence to support the conclusion that treating children as consumers is harmful.

(b) This is a counter-argument that advertising to children can have positive effects.

(c) This is an intermediate conclusion, supported by reasoning throughout the article.

Question 2

Identify the structure of the reasoning in paragraph 5. (12 marks)

■ ■ ■

Model answer

R1 is that many poor parents will be working hard, with no choice, just to put food on the table.

Example: Some will be cleaning your house or looking after your children.

R2 is that few can afford a house with a garden.

R1 + R2 (reasons work together) support IC1, which is that you cannot just blame the parents. (This is a response to an anticipated counter-argument that parents, rather than television, are to blame.)

CA: There then follows a counter-argument from Baroness Buscombe that advertising can be a social good and can lead to healthier lifestyles. The author responds to this CA as follows:

R3: Advertising exists to sell things — toys, dreams, promises. That's all.

IC2: It is overwhelmingly damaging (R3 supports IC2).

Evaluation questions

Evaluate the reasoning in paragraphs 1–6. (10 marks)

■ ■ ■

Model answer

Appeal to history: We learn that things were different in the time of the author's childhood. The appeal to history can only strengthen her argument if it is shown to be relevant (otherwise it becomes an 'irrelevant appeal to history'). The author does say that she did not feel deprived, but this is a hasty generalisation from a single example. The evidence in paragraph 2 does not show that children were happier in the past than they are today, or that eating habits or attention spans have actually worsened. Thus the appeal to history is irrelevant.

Use of evidence: In the second paragraph, the author uses evidence from the Children's Society that one in ten children now has a mental illness diagnosed. However, just because diagnoses are increasing, it does not automatically follow that mental illnesses are increasing, since it may just be the *diagnoses* of mental illnesses that are on the increase.

The Children's Society has suggested that 'materialistic consumer pressure may be partly to blame'. The weakness here is that a conclusion is being drawn from inconclusive evidence. However, the phrase 'may be partly to blame' suggests that the Children's Society is not prepared to say that materialistic consumer pressure is certainly to blame and that, even if it is, it is only one cause among others. The author is much less cautious in interpreting this evidence, rejecting other explanations.

Inconsistency: The author claims that the consumer pressure comes 'first from television'. She fails to say what the other sources are until paragraph 6. Here, she seems to say that school friends and celebrity excess are the main culprits and that television exacerbates this problem, which is not the same thing as saying that television is the primary root of the problem. Therefore, there could be said to be an inconsistency between paragraphs 3 and 6.

Gardens: The author has reasoned that, because poor families are less likely to have gardens, it necessarily follows that children in poor families are likely to watch more television. The author's reasoning is that not having a garden leads to more time spent indoors and more time spent indoors results in more time watching television. This reasoning is plausible but it would be strengthened if it could be supported with evidence that there really is a connection between not having a garden and watching more television. It is possible that children living in homes without gardens may go elsewhere (e.g. to a playground or shopping centre).

Advertising: Finally, the author considers a further counter-argument from Baroness Buscombe that advertising to children can be a social good, among other things contributing to healthier lifestyles. The author's response is that this cannot be the case because the function of advertising is to sell things. This reasoning may seem to be inadequate because it ignores the possibility that some advertising can be public service advertising and that commercial advertising could be socially responsible. Just because advertising would not exist without a desire to sell things, it does not automatically follow that no social good can possibly result. The author fails to support her strong claim that all advertising exists simply to sell things and can therefore do no social good.

Inconsistency: Having rejected the counter-assertion that parents are to blame, the author acknowledges, at the beginning of paragraph 6, that 'parents can correct bouts of consumerism in their children'. This could be said to be inconsistent with her earlier reasoning.

Evaluate the reasoning in the remainder of this argument. (paragraphs 7–15) (10 marks)

■ ■ ■

Model answer

Needs and wants: In paragraph 7, the author seems to reason that television advertising is undesirable because we could live without it. She distinguishes between needs and wants. It is clear that human beings could indeed survive without television advertising, but that does not seem to be a strong argument to support a position that television advertising is undesirable.

Rights: The author claims that Lady Buscombe's argument relies on an assumption that children have a right to consumer choice. If it is true that Lady Buscombe believes that children have a right to consumer choice, then the author's counter-argument is weak. In paragraph 8, the author argues that it is not necessarily in our interests to have choice, but this would not address an argument that we have a right to choose. Rights exist whether or not exercising them is always in the interests of those who hold them. The right to choose means the right to make the wrong choices.

Examples: The author offers four examples of choices that could be seen as stressful and confusing and these would have to be considered in turn. We should ask to what extent they are indeed stressful and confusing and also whether or not the author would be sympathetic to the idea that such choices should be removed. Choosing a school could, for example, be much more stressful than choosing a brand of yoghurt. Is the author seriously suggesting that only one brand of yoghurt should be available? If so, this would seem to be an argument for rigid state control of the economy and the weakness of this, in the context of this passage, is that the author would seem to be deviating from her main argument.

Inconsistency: In paragraphs 8–9, the author seems to be arguing that the right to choose is bad for everyone, children and adults alike. The question of whether or not this means that she would want to deny adults the right to choose is unanswered in her argument. Either the author believes that no one has a right to consumer choice or else she must assume that the right to consumer choice that is held by adults should not extend to children. Her argument is weakened because this reasoning is unclear.

Slippery slope: In paragraphs 11–12, there is a dramatic slippery slope, where the author goes too far too quickly. She reasons that consumer choice will lead to disappointed consumers who will then hang morosely around shopping centres and will then be 'buzzed off' by Mosquito devices and will then demand Prozac from doctors to deal with their depression. Slippery slopes are when a chain of events suggests that one thing will inevitably lead to another and disaster will result. The reasoning that one thing will necessarily lead to another is suspect and not supported with evidence.

Inconsistency: In the final paragraph, the author concludes that we are spoilt and that we are spoiling our children. The author has supported this intermediate conclusion with reasoning that children in the modern age have far more choice than previous generations and that television advertising presents a range of choices, but her argument relies on the presupposition that, especially for children in poor families, some choices are unattainable. Therefore, far from being spoilt, the problem that she has identified is that many people cannot have everything that they want, hence the morose disaffected youths hanging around shopping centres.

Conclusion: The author then appears to draw a conclusion that children should be taught differently but her argument is weakened by her failure to explain who should be doing the teaching. Earlier in her argument, she argued that some parents, especially poor parents, could not reasonably be expected to teach this lesson.

Evaluate the effectiveness of the following counter-arguments in responding to the author's argument. (10 marks)

(a)

You may be described by some as looking through rose-tinted glasses at your past, but perhaps you would be right to do that.

Children being targeted as consumers by marketing forces is unfortunate but inevitable. Consumerism, for all its evils, is the control method of a liberal government. We cannot legitimately use force to control the masses so we use consumerism. The man walking down the street becomes consumed with the thoughts of what mobile phone he can buy next, or which tiles would make his bathroom better than his neighbours. It is better that he thinks this than is aware that he is not as free as he thought, and tries to take something from you or rebel against society.

At least we are free to rise above materialism and consumerism, if we are able to see past its trappings. We are also free to protect our children from it by switching off the TV.

Richard Tomlin, Nottingham

(b)

OK then, I deny you the option of having less choice. Happy now?

Felix, Nottingham

■ ■ ■

Model answer

The first paragraph of Passage (a) does not really damage the author's argument. Tomlin notes that Miles may be making an appeal to history but acknowledges that it may be a relevant appeal.

Tomlin's counter-argument is that consumer choice is the result of a free liberal economy, in which consumer choice is a right, at least for adults. The author explores the reasons for such rights and where they arise from, which could be said to be more convincing than the reasoning of Miles. Rights, such as the right to choose, may make life more complicated and stressful but does this necessarily mean that we would be better off without these rights?

In the final paragraph, Tomlin suggests that the solution to the problem is to protect children by restricting their television viewing. This does not effectively counter the author's argument because she has already anticipated and responded to this counter-argument, although she may have been guilty of some inconsistency.

In Passage (b), Felix asks a loaded question that raises the question of how Miles might respond if she were compelled to have choice. The question is effective in suggesting the possibility that her least favoured option might be imposed on her, if she were to be denied the right to choose.

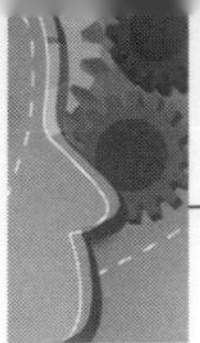

Sample B

Resource booklet

It's no surprise children have retreated into a techno-Narnia

Alice has moved on. Today's child has access to a world more perplexing than the 1
universe Lewis Carroll's heroine found beneath the rabbit hole. The modern version of the story of a pre-teenager lost in a fantasy realm could be entitled *Alice in Cyberspace*.

Earlier this week, research by the Institute of Public Policy Research warned Britons 2
are 'being raised online'. Youngsters spend more than 20 hours a week in a virtual life, chiefly on social networking sites, such as Facebook, MySpace and Bebo.

Dr Tanya Byron, a child psychologist and television presenter, will launch her 3
much-anticipated report. Byron, commissioned by Gordon Brown to review online risks and video games, wants a 'national strategy for child internet safety', in which the Government undertakes both to teach parents about computer literacy and to issue tough rules to industry.

'Web 2.0', or social networking sites, should, in Byron's view, be compelled to 4
apply rigorous security measures, such as privacy standards, and be tightly regulated. The classification of computer games must be overhauled. Ministers have already conceded privately they will do exactly what Byron asks. Although she emphasises the benefits of the internet, the risks she identifies will inflame existing fears of a cyber-domain containing horrors undreamed of by Carroll's heroine.

Where Old Alice had merely to cope with a Mad Hatter, New Alice may be negoti- 5
ating the Miss Bimbo website, on which pre-pubescent girls are encouraged to keep their virtual characters 'waif thin' with diet pills and buy them breast implant surgery. For violence, Old Alice saw the Queen of Hearts screeching for blood. Her modern equivalent can watch real-life happy slappings on YouTube. One recent scene of brutality, entitled 'Girl Beat Up In Street', had 1,300,000 hits.

No wonder the suspicion is growing that the internet is the lonely, threatening 6
habitat of bullies and predators. The modern Wonderland stands accused by many of inciting narcissism, idleness, obesity and even suicide. While Byron argues children are also being 'empowered', doom-mongers are unlikely to be so sanguine.

Cultural pessimists, however, have often been wrong. For example, the warning by 7
the media theorist Marshall McLuhan that new technology would kill off books ushered in a publishing boom in which Virginia Woolf has not been wholly supplanted by the literary oeuvres of football WAGS. Serious subjects, such as history, also make bestsellers.

Far from being dumbed down by the information age, we are smartening up. Jim Flynn, a New Zealand professor, has charted year-on-year rises in IQ scores across the world, and tests show that Britons' average IQ has risen 27 points since 1942. True, school leavers might know nothing of Clement Attlee or the nine-times table, but that's the fault of our education system. The cognitive labour demanded by games and assimilating detail is linked to better mental dexterity. Our brains have been reprogrammed. 8

But the internet also causes problems the Government failed to foresee when it first embraced the 'knowledge economy' and the educational benefits of computers. As Kay Withers's IPPR report recalls, £6 million was invested to ensure schools got broadband and so escaped 'the technological dark ages'. There was no mention then of parenting classes in new technology, or of forcing unscrupulous operators to stop selling vile computer games to small children. Though any suggestion that screen brutality triggers violence in children is unproved, as Byron allows, most people would agree that the internet has scope to alter vulnerable minds. 9

If the Government is reaping what it sowed, then parents are also in line for blame. As well as being a must-have learning tool, computers have become a diversion from the perilous outdoors. The street-corner paedophile, mostly a figment of over-anxious adult imagination, has mutated into the more pernicious web-stalker. Some children, far from being passive recipients of violence, are posting scenes of thuggery online. Others, by flaunting their identity, or posting drunken portraits on MySpace, are courting dangers peculiar to the online world. In our safety-obsessed society, risk has come home to roost. 10

Children are supposedly culprits, too. 'Frankenkinder', spoilt, undisciplined brats bribed with games consoles, are the latest social curse to cross the Atlantic. Fear of 'bad' children, and the monsters that beset them, is as old as fairytales. Even so, something odd is happening. This is a century in which the gap between adults and children has, supposedly, been wiped out by the 'kidult'; the Botoxed adult with hip-hop on the iPod and eternal youth in mind. Yet, at a time when adults have little or no knowledge of what their children do in cyberspace, the chasm between old and young has rarely been so wide. Previous gulfs between generations, such as views on sex and music, have been replaced by the digital divide. 11

Byron, who will personally deliver her report to Gordon Brown, is calling for a 'social marketing campaign'. Though no one is going to argue with a plea for more awareness and better safety, the limited power of the state to influence behaviour runs particularly thin in cyberspace. 12

Let us, by all means, have a clampdown on a dodgy industry and computer classes for grown-ups. Even if we cannot persuade our children to take up jigsaw puzzles, we will be better at ordering our Tesco shopping online. But equipping children to thrive on the internet cannot be learned from any social rulebook or state-sponsored seminars in geekishness. 13

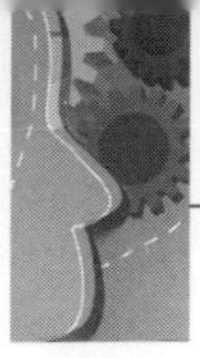

Online security is best taught in the offline universe. That means giving children, of 14
whom one in 10 has never been read a bedtime story, more parental time. It means teaching them that gratuitous cruelty is as insupportable in the virtual as in the real world. It means stopping sapping children's happiness by plying them with alcohol and junk food, or testing them to destruction in schools that too often offer a shameful education. But it also means crushing some adult myths of lost innocence.

As Robin Alexander, who is heading the Primary Review of education, hinted last 15
week, we don't have a crisis of childhood. We have a crisis of alarmism. There is a risk that the Byron report, however sensible, will unleash that panic.

Children have always been seen as prey, at the mercy of any demon invented by 16
adults. Just as the wolf did not kill Red Riding Hood, the big bad internet will not swallow up our babies. Some of its risks are avoidable and unacceptable. But children, resourceful and resilient, have always sought a private world, free from adult scrutiny. When playing fields are concreted over, playgrounds deemed out-of-bounds and youngsters plagued either by failure or the pressure to succeed, it's not surprising they retreat into a techno-Narnia.

Parents and politicians cannot make this world wholly safe. Maybe the best they 17
can offer, for all the talk of education and crackdowns, is to equip children better to deal with hazards placed in their way by adults. Byron's findings sound moderate and balanced. That may not defuse a media firestorm about the (largely unproved) evils of the internet. As the Queen shouted across the courtroom where Alice sat: 'Sentence first — verdict afterwards.'

Source: Mary Riddell © Telegraph Media Group Ltd (27 March 2008)

Question 1

Analysis questions

Identify and briefly explain the function of the following elements in the structure of the argument:

(a) 'Alice has moved on. Today's child has access to a world more perplexing than the universe Lewis Carroll's heroine found beneath the rabbit hole.' (paragraph 1) (2 marks)

(b) 'Youngsters spend more than 20 hours a week in a virtual life, chiefly on social networking sites, such as Facebook, MySpace and Bebo.' (paragraph 2) (2 marks)

(c) '...New Alice may be negotiating the Miss Bimbo website, on which pre-pubescent girls are encouraged to keep their virtual characters "waif thin" with diet pills and buy them breast implant surgery.' (paragraph 5) (2 marks)

(d) '...it's not surprising they retreat into a techno-Narnia.' (paragraph 16) (2 marks)

■ ■ ■

Model answers

(a) This is scene-setting material, which is not part of the argument itself. *Alice in Wonderland* is used as an example of a perplexing universe, which children might inhabit. The author claims that the modern online world is even more perplexing than *Alice in Wonderland*.

(b) This is evidence, used to support the claim that Britons are 'being raised online'.

(c) The Miss Bimbo website is used as an example of risks on the internet.

(d) This is an intermediate conclusion.

Analyse in detail the structure of the reasoning in paragraph 9. (12 marks)

■ ■ ■

Model answer

The author starts with an intermediate conclusion, that the internet causes problems that the government failed to foresee.

This intermediate conclusion is supported with a reason and with evidence. The evidence is the IPPR report, which recalls that £6m was invested to ensure that schools got broadband internet access. The reason is that, at the time of this investment, the government did not mention the need for parenting classes or for restricting the sale of 'vile computer games' to small children.

There is then a counterclaim that the link between screen brutality and violence in children is unproved.

In response to this counterclaim, the author says that 'most people would agree' that the internet can alter vulnerable minds.

The author's response is supported by evidence of some support from Byron.

IC: 'But the internet also causes problems the Government failed to foresee...'

Evidence: 'As Kay Withers's IPPR report recalls, £6 million was invested to ensure that schools got broadband...'

Reason: 'There was no mention then of parenting classes in new technology, or of forcing unscrupulous operators to stop selling vile computer games to small children.'

Counterclaim: 'Though any suggestion that screen brutality triggers violence in children is unproved...'

Evidence: '...as Byron allows...'

Response to counterclaim: 'Most people would agree that the internet has scope to alter vulnerable minds.'

Evaluation questions

Evaluate the strength of the author's reasoning in paragraphs 1–9. How strong is the support for the claim that 'the internet has scope to alter vulnerable minds'? (10 marks)

■ ■ ■

Model answer

Evidence: In paragraph 2, the author offers evidence of a warning, from the Institute of Public Policy Research, that Britons are 'being raised online'. Youngsters spend more than 20 hours a week online, chiefly on social networking sites. This evidence shows that the average child is spending a great deal of time online but the claim that children are 'being raised online' would seem to be hyperbolic exaggeration.

Examples: In paragraphs 5–6, examples are given of the 'horrors' that children might encounter on the internet. The Miss Bimbo website and the YouTube happy slapping videos are supposed to explain why many people (the author does not necessarily include herself) believe that the internet is, 'the lonely, threatening habitat of bullies and predators' and that it incites 'narcissism, idleness, obesity and even suicide'. Neither example illustrates how children might become victims of predators. If idleness and obesity result, it would be from the amount of time spent online (the 20 hours a week claim) rather than the particular websites looked at. Other problems, such as those of narcissism and suicide could be linked to cyber-bullying and the long-term psychological effects of websites such as Miss Bimbo. However, the author has accepted elsewhere (paragraph 9) that there is no conclusive evidence to support a link between what children see and what they do, rather she is appealing to popular opinion in citing growing suspicions and accusations, and referring to what 'most people' think, without saying whether or not she shares these views.

Appeal to history: In paragraph 7, there is an appeal to history, to remind us that cultural pessimists have often been wrong before, but that is no guarantee that they will be proved wrong this time. The author then claims that 'our brains have been reprogrammed', citing the evidence that IQ scores across the world have been increasing, and she claims a link between the 'cognitive labour' demanded by computer games and 'better mental dexterity'. The problem with this evidence is that there are many alternative explanations for why IQ scores are increasing, such as better diet, better education or inaccuracy of the tests. A problem with the author's explanation is that, if scores have been increasing since 1942, there must have been some other factor at work before computer games and the internet became popular.

Conflation: The author has conflated computer games and use of the internet, in that she treats them almost as if they were the same thing. Furthermore, she fails to distinguish between school and home internet use. Few, if any, schools will encourage

the playing of violent computer games and a great many will filter such sites as YouTube and Miss Bimbo. Indeed, most of the problems identified by the author will be connected to use of computers in the home, so the author's claim that the government has reaped what it has sowed could be seen as weak.

Overall, the author has shown that the evidence that computer games or the internet can alter minds, either for better or worse, is inconclusive.

Question 4

Evaluate the author's reasoning in paragraphs 10–17. To what extent does the author's reasoning support the claims that '...we don't have a crisis of childhood. We have a crisis of alarmism...' and that Byron's report could unleash panic? (10 marks)

■ ■ ■

Model answer

Inconsistency/examples/use of evidence: Although the author concludes (in paragraphs 15–17) that there is a crisis of alarmism rather than a crisis of childhood, much of the reasoning in the remainder of her argument could be seen as being inconsistent with this conclusion, for example:

- Paragraph 10: The author says that, although the traditional street-corner paedophile was mostly a figment of adult imagination, the modern web-stalker is more pernicious. If true, this would seem to be inconsistent with the author's reasoning that parents should not be worried about their children retreating into a private world because children in the past did something similar without coming to harm.
- Paragraph 10: Some children are courting danger by flaunting their identity on MySpace.
- Paragraph 10: Some children are posting scenes of thuggery online. This would seem to be something that should concern parents whether their children are the thugs or the victims.
- Paragraph 11: Some children are undisciplined 'Frankenkinder' brats.
- Paragraph 11: The chasm between young and old has rarely been so wide.
- Paragraph 14: One in ten children has never been read a bedtime story. This evidence is intended to show that some parents are not devoting enough time to interacting with their children but the figure does not show whether this problem has got any worse.
- Paragraph 14: The author suggests that there is a problem of parents sapping children's happiness by plying them with junk food and alcohol.
- Paragraph 14: Schools, too often, offer a shameful education and children are being 'tested to destruction'.

The author agrees that there are benefits and dangers associated with computer games and the internet but, overall, she has given more examples of dangers than benefits. She has given several strong examples of serious problems in modern childhood that would seem to be inconsistent with her conclusion that the real problem is a crisis of alarmism.

The numerous alarmist examples offered by the author (only some of which are connected with computer games and the internet) weaken her conclusion, rather than strengthening it.

The author's conclusion (paragraph 17) is that Byron's report is sensible and balanced but that it could also 'unleash panic' in the form of 'a media firestorm about the

(largely unproved) evils of the internet'. Although she believes that media panic is almost inevitable, she disassociates herself from this alarmism.

Appeal to history: In paragraph 16, the author claims that children have always been seen as prey, at the mercy of demons invented by adults and the wolf in Little Red Riding Hood is given as an example of an invented risk that did not cause the deaths of children. The weakness in this reasoning is that, because some risks have been invented in the past, it does not necessarily follow that the dangers of the present are not worth worrying about.

Inconsistency: In paragraph 16, the author accepts that some risks are 'avoidable and unacceptable' and she responds to this concern by claiming that children are 'resourceful and resilient'. If the dangers of the internet are unacceptable, it should follow that the resourcefulness and resilience of children are insufficient to protect all of them from danger.

Appeal to history: In paragraph 16, the author makes a further appeal to history in observing that children have always sought a private world free from adult scrutiny. The author also argues that, as playing fields and playgrounds are no longer accessible to children, it is unsurprising that they should seek some other private world. Her intention is to show that we should not be unduly alarmed that children should want to retreat into an online world that is not understood by adults. A criticism could be that, just because children may be naturally inclined to seek a private world, it does not necessarily follow that parents should not be very concerned about what they might be up to (the author seems to confuse 'is' and 'ought').

Sample C

Resource booklet

Background information

John Humphrys interviewed Mr Tomato Lichy (a 'deaf activist') on Radio 4's *Today* programme on 10 March 2008.

Lichy and his partner are both deaf and they already have a deaf child. They now want to try for a second child using IVF (in vitro fertilisation). IVF is a process by which egg cells are fertilised outside the womb. This has sometimes been called 'test tube baby' technology.

During an IVF process, several embryos are created and one or two will be selected for implantation. The selected embryo will normally be the one most likely to be successful in developing into a foetus.

If it were possible to tell which embryo(s) were likely to be born deaf, Tomato Lichy would like the right to choose a deaf child. The government, however, would like to prohibit such a choice.

During the interview, John Humphrys accused Tomato Lichy of wanting to impose a serious disability on a child. In response, Lichy argued that he did not regard deafness as a disability.

Of course a deaf couple want a deaf child

It is not as if the implantation of an embryo thought to be deaf is equivalent to mutilation

Few broadcasters convey astonishment with an undertone of outrage as skilfully as 1
the BBC's John Humphrys. Over the years the *Today* programme presenter has had a lot of practice. Yesterday, however, it was not an equivocating politician who got Humphrys to hit his top note. It was a bloke called Tomato — Mr Tomato Lichy, to be precise. The programme's listeners never actually heard Mr Lichy speak: he responded to John Humphrys' questions in sign language, and someone else turned his answers into spoken English for the interviewer's — and our — benefit.

Tomato Lichy and his partner Paula are both deaf. They have a deaf child, Molly. 2
Now Paula is in her 40s and the couple believe they might require IVF treatment to produce a second child. They very much want such a child also to be deaf.

Here's where it gets political: the Government is whipping through a new Human 3
Fertilisation and Embryology Bill. Clause 14/4/9 states that, 'Persons or embryos that are known to have a gene, chromosome or mitochondrion abnormality

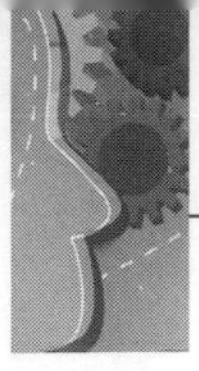

involving a significant risk that a person with the abnormality will have or develop a serious physical or mental disability, a serious illness or any other serious medical condition must not be preferred to those that are not known to have such an abnormality'.

This, Tomato Lichy signed to Mr Humphrys, means that he and his partner would 4
be compelled by law to discard the very embryos that they wished to have implanted: 'I couldn't participate in any procedure which forced me to reject a deaf embryo in favour of a hearing embryo.' Mr Lichy argued that this legislation was specifically designed to discriminate against deafness. As a matter of fact, he's quite right.

The explanatory notes to the clause inform legislators: 'Outside the UK, the posi- 5
tive selection of deaf donors in order deliberately to result in a deaf child has been reported. This provision would prevent (embryo) selection for a similar purpose.' This all stems from a single case in the US six years ago, when a lesbian couple, Sharon Duchesneau and Candace McCullough, both of whom were deaf, selected a sperm donor on the basis of his family history of deafness. It caused outrage — outrage which clearly filtered through to the British Health ministry.

The most revealing account of this most unusual conception appeared in an email 6
interview in the Lancet. Duchesneau and McCullough wrote: 'Most of the ethical issues that have been raised in regard to our story centre on the idea that being deaf is a negative thing. From there, people surmise that it is unethical to want to create deaf children, who are, in their view, disabled.

'Our view, on the other hand, is that being deaf is a positive thing, with many won- 7
derful aspects. We don't view being deaf along the same lines as being blind or mentally retarded; we see it as paralleling being Jewish or black. We don't see members of those minority groups wanting to eliminate themselves.'

This is as clear an exposition as you will see of the concept of 'cultural deafness'. 8
Adherents of this philosophy refer not just to 'deaf culture' — Mr Lichy said he felt 'sorry for' John Humphrys for not being able to appreciate 'deaf plays' — but to themselves as members of a 'linguistic community'. This idea of a separate language enables the proponents of cultural deafness to describe themselves as, in effect, an ethnic minority — and thus any legislative attempt to weed them out as embryos to be analogous with the most insidious racism.

Another deaf British couple, whose child is also deaf, told the BBC's disability mag- 9
azine that 'it is important that our culture is passed on from one generation to another...the threat of losing our culture would be devastating because we have so much to show and to give'.

In the most obvious sense, the argument that deafness is not a disability is self- 10
evidently wrong. The absence of one of our most valuable senses brings with it many disadvantages on a purely practical level. So many careers are all but closed to the deaf — a deaf boy might well have fantasies about being a soldier or a

fireman, but fantasies are what they will remain. Humphrys tasked Tomato Lichy with the fact that he would never be able to enjoy the music of Beethoven — a low blow, this, as Beethoven himself was vilely tormented by increasing deafness, which also put an end to his ability to conduct his own music.

Yet I don't share Humphrys' apparent incredulity at his interviewee's dismissal of the joys of music. If you have never been able to hear music, then you cannot be said to miss it, or suffer from its absence from your life. Indeed, I know one or two people who are completely tone deaf, who are not in the least miserable about it: their only irritation is in occasionally having to hear what to them is just undifferentiated noise, when they would rather have silence. The idea that congenitally deaf people are 'suffering' in some intrinsic sense, strikes me as mere presumption. 11

Moreover, it is not as if the implantation of an embryo which is thought likely to be deaf — and science at the moment would be very hard pushed to forecast such an outcome with any reliability at all — is equivalent to deliberate mutilation. What we are talking about is an already existing potential person; the choice isn't whether that embryo could be 'made deaf' or not. The choice is whether to discard that already existing embryo for another one believed to be less at risk of turning out to be deaf. 12

Given that the fertilisation process within IVF generates many more test-tube embryos than are selected for implantation, there are always going to be vast quantities of 'normal' embryos which will be destroyed. 13

The real issue here, as Mr Lichy observed, is whether the state should be able to dictate to him and his partner which of their embryos they should be allowed to select, and which they should be compelled to reject. I am not surprised — still less, incredulous — that he can't understand why he and his partner should be prevented by law from choosing the embryo which might most turn out to resemble them. 14

John Humphrys argued that most people would regard his demands as profoundly selfish: Mr Lichy and his partner might want a deaf child, but what about the views of the child itself? I suspect that the child in question would be intelligent enough to be able to understand that the only alternative deal for him or her was never to have existed at all. 15

Nevertheless, if Clause 14 of the HFE Bill does pass into law, I do hope that Mr Lichy and his partner will find it in them to love and cherish a child who is not deaf. We hearing people are not so useless, when you get to know us properly. 16

Source: Dominic Lawson © the *Independent* (11 March 2008)

Analysis questions

Identify and briefly explain the function of the following elements in the structure of this argument:

(a) 'In the most obvious sense, the argument that deafness is not a disability is self-evidently wrong.' (paragraph 10) (2 marks)

(b) 'Indeed, I know one or two people who are completely tone deaf, who are not in the least miserable about it...' (paragraph 11) (2 marks)

(c) 'I suspect that the child in question would be intelligent enough to be able to understand that the only alternative deal for him or her was never to have existed at all.' (paragraph 15) (2 marks)

■ ■ ■

Model answers

(a) This is the conclusion of a counter-argument.

(b) This is evidence used to support the author's response to the counter-argument in paragraph 10.

(c) This is a response to a counter-argument. The counter-argument (in the preceding paragraph) is that Lichy's deaf child might resent him for imposing deafness on him.

Identify the structure of the reasoning in paragraph 8. (12 marks)

■ ■ ■

Model answer

There are two reasons, which work together to support an intermediate conclusion. The first reason is that there is such a thing as deaf culture, with deaf plays being offered as an example. The second reason is that there is a separate deaf language (sign language), so deaf people could be regarded as a 'linguistic community'.

Because deaf people have their own culture (R1) and their own language (R2), the author reasons that they are, therefore, like (analogous to) an ethnic minority (IC).

The author then reasons that, if deaf people are like an ethnic minority, an attempt to eradicate their group would be like the worst sort of racism.

R1: There is such a thing as a deaf culture.

Example: Hearing people cannot appreciate deaf plays.

R2: Deaf people are a linguistic community because there is a separate language.

IC: Deaf people are, in effect, an ethnic minority.

C: Therefore, any legislative attempt to weed them out as embryos would be analogous with the most insidious racism.

Evaluation questions

Evaluate the author's reasoning, in paragraphs 7–9. How effectively does the author support his argument that the government is discriminating against deaf people in a way that is 'analogous with...racism'? (10 marks)

■ ■ ■

Model answer

Assumption/principle: It is clear that there is such a thing as a 'deaf culture' with a separate language, deaf plays, deaf jokes and so on. In order to make his argument, the author must assume that the existence of this culture is a positive thing and that it is important for it to be preserved and passed from generation to generation. Maybe the author is confusing 'is' and 'ought' in reasoning that the existence of a separate culture necessarily makes that culture desirable. An alternative view would be that the separate deaf culture exists because deaf people are excluded from the wider culture and that deaf people are disadvantaged by being so excluded.

Examples: The author offers two examples to support his view that deaf people have a separate culture. Deaf plays and the deaf language (sign language) are strong examples of cultural separateness from which hearing people are excluded. These examples are strong enough to support the concept of 'cultural deafness' but may not be strong enough to support the analogy that deaf people are like an ethnic minority.

Straw man: It is certainly true that to seek to eliminate an ethnic group by stopping people reproducing would be insidious racism but is that really what the government is proposing for the deaf? Most deaf people are conceived naturally, rather than by IVF, and the government is not proposing the prevention of natural conceptions. In distorting the government's position, the author could be accused of seeking to attack a straw man. However, the author could be seen to be reasonable in making the charge of discrimination in the case of IVF. If deaf embryos should, wherever possible, be discarded, then it is reasonable to conclude that deafness is regarded as a negative thing and thus undesirable. Furthermore, if hearing embryos are to be selected in preference to deaf ones, then it would seem to be reasonable for the author to conclude that the government is proposing discrimination.

Inconsistency: The alleged discrimination is in actively choosing deaf embryos over hearing ones, with both parties favouring discrimination. In an IVF procedure, several embryos will be created and the 'best' one will be selected for implantation. Activists such as Tomato Lichy would be in favour of deaf people discriminating against hearing embryos. Therefore, it would seem that the author is not against all discrimination but he believes that the discrimination should be parental choice rather than being dictated by the government.

Analogy: The author is not saying that deaf people are an ethnic minority; rather he is saying that an analogy can be drawn between the deaf community and an ethnic minority group. Similarities would be that deaf people have a separate and distinct culture and their own language. A further similarity would be that an attempt to 'eliminate' or 'weed out' their group would be clear discrimination. A major difference is that, in any IVF procedure, the embryos are all from the same ethnic group and, so, the government could not attempt to 'weed out' embryos from any one race.

Overall, the success of the author's argument depends on the strength or weakness of the analogy that compares the deaf community with an ethnic minority.

…n Humphrys argued that Tomato Lichy's choice was 'selfish' because he would be 'imposing' deafness on a child. Evaluate the effectiveness of the author's response to these counter-arguments in paragraphs 10–16. (10 marks)

■ ■ ■

Model answer

The counter-arguments are:

- Deafness is clearly a disability.
- Lichy wants to 'impose' deafness on a child.
- Lichy's choice is 'selfish'.

Examples: In paragraphs 10–11, the author's reasoning is that deaf people are not disabled because they are not suffering. He considers the counter-argument that deafness prevents deaf people from doing certain things and there are several relevant examples offered. Deaf people are prevented from entering careers such as the fire service and the armed forces and they cannot hear music. The author addresses the example of deaf people not being able to hear music with the reasoning that if they have never been able to hear music then they cannot suffer through missing it. His other examples, however, would seem to weaken this reasoning. For example, a young boy who dreams of being a soldier has not experienced being a soldier but he may still regret not being able to achieve his dream.

Straw man?: John Humphrys did not use the phrase 'deliberate mutilation' but he did say that Lichy wanted to 'impose' deafness on a child. The author's response is to show that Lichy does not want to do any such thing. In wanting to choose a deaf embryo, Lichy does not want to impose deafness on a child who would otherwise be able to hear. The author is quite successful in showing that the potential hearing child and the potential deaf child are two different children.

Consistency: In paragraph 14, the author states that the 'real issue' is whether the state or the parents should be allowed to select between the available embryos. The government would seem to be saying that it is preferable for deaf parents to, wherever possible, have a hearing child. In disagreeing with the government's position, the author is relying on the earlier reasoning in his argument, that deafness is not a negative thing or a disability.

Sample D

Resource booklet

Background information

Paul Gascoigne (Gazza) is a retired English football player, widely regarded as one of the most naturally talented footballers of his generation. He played for Newcastle, Spurs, Lazio and Glasgow Rangers and was capped 57 times for England. After he came to prominence in Italia '90, many stories about Gazza's pranks, drinking and domestic problems featured in the tabloid press. In February 2008, he was taken into protective custody under the terms of the Mental Health Act.

George Best (1946–2005) is often regarded as one of the greatest football players of all time, although, as a Northern Ireland international, he never played in a World Cup. Best came to prominence in the 1960s and is notable for being, arguably, the first celebrity footballer. He opened fashion boutiques and nightclubs and was notorious for his womanising and drinking. He refused to give up drinking, even after receiving a liver transplant. After he died in 2005, 100,000 people turned out for his funeral on a rainy day in East Belfast.

For women, Gazza isn't a fallen hero. He's a sad drunk

This is no Greek epic, just the hackneyed old tale of an alcoholic

There is always a precise point, during the self-induced decline of a great sporting 1
hero, when men become helplessly misty eyed and women completely lose sympathy both with the cause and those who do the lamenting.

We saw it with George Best and we are seeing it again with Paul Gascoigne, the 2
former football star who has been sectioned under the Mental Health Act, allegedly after a two-month drink and drugs bender in a series of four-star hotels where he has been resident.

The immediate response, from Britain's excitable male, middle-aged sports com- 3
mentators — and I exclude my colleague Simon Barnes from the list of shame — was to tell us all the sordid details and interpret Gascoigne's fall as the latest episode of a Greek tragedy. For the rest of us, however, there wasn't anything the least bit epic about it.

Funny, isn't it? The female sex, which adores romance in all its forms, and melts 4
with desire for your average fallen titan, especially if he's called Mr Rochester, simply isn't touched by the drama of this shattered genius.

That's largely because we don't perceive Gazza as a shattered genius at all, but as 5

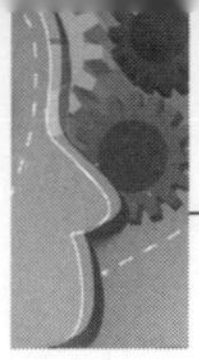

an alcoholic predictably ruined by his own addiction. Along, it has to be said, with several hundred thousand other people in Britain, many of whom had many fewer chances in life than he had.

There is sympathy. Of course there is. At a human level, one can only feel sorry for a man so sick and isolated that he lives alone, long term, in posh hotels for as long as they will have him, playing computer games and drinking to the point where his behaviour becomes unsustainable. 6

But what there should not be is lionisation. Or lack of honesty. What troubles me about the whole Gazza saga, which will surely run until the poor chap is finally at peace, is the extraordinary sense of denial by football fans over what has brought him to this new low. 7

The answer, I have little doubt, is alcohol addiction, the most bog-standard, unglamorous, mundane, miserable, destructive, grievous kind of affliction you can get. The one as common as the common cold. 8

The one people shy away from discussing because it's often just too close to their own domestic circumstances. Understandably, but wrongly, those who seek to romanticise the catastrophe of the great star Gazza don't want his plight to be due to anything as ordinary as booze. But it is. 9

What depresses me about the focus on the fact that he was sectioned under the Mental Health Act is that this will become the red herring, the get-out clause. Ah, Gazza's mad, that's the problem. He's had a breakdown. He's psychotic. It's his demons. 10

In other words, it's nothing to do with alcohol; it's because he's got something wrong with his head. Ergo: we can go on drinking as much as we like. 11

I know no more about Gascoigne's health than I read in the media. But I doubt that this is a story about sudden mental breakdown. Instead, this is the common-or-garden story of what happens if you spend your life, as Gascoigne has famously done, constantly drinking double and treble measures of spirits at various points in the day in order to acquire the desired level of anaesthesia. 12

The anecdotes tell of how he would sneak into the boardrooms of football clubs immediately before the big games and throw double whiskies down his throat. On the occasion when he confessed to beating up his wife in Gleneagles Hotel, leaving her with broken fingers and a black eye, he had spent the night drinking treble brandies. And over the years, as his youth and fitness declined, and his body refused to cope any more, he went to be dried out several times. 13

When chronic drinkers get to 40, as Gascoigne is now, many are showing signs of brain damage. Alcohol related brain damage (ARBD), the doctors call it, when years of heavy drinking start to attack the nervous functions. Research shows that 82 per cent of down-and-outs, of whatever age, have cognitive impairment from alcohol. 14

Everyone knows someone. Everyone can look among their own contemporaries to 15
those who drank heavily when they were young but forgot to stop. Or listen to young, deranged street drunks, many of whom are now displaying symptoms of ARBD in their twenties.

'Pure dead mental', as they say in Glasgow, admiringly, of deranged, alcohol- 16
induced behaviour. Is it any wonder that the Rangers fans recognised Gazza as one of their own? In their terms, long before the psychiatrists examined him, he was 'pure mental'.

ARBD is characterised by volatile behaviour, short-term memory loss, failure of 17
reasoning power, inability to store information or monitor repetitious talk and inability to take control of one's life. Nobody has to be an expert in alcohol, in other words, to understand that after years of alcohol abuse people's personalities start to disintegrate.

Personally, I see no Greek tragedy in Gascoigne's chaos. I feel as sorry for him as I 18
do for any damaged, addicted person. The man had great talent and must, at his peak, have earned enough to buy out the local bank. But he was weak, not heroic. He lacked either a sense of responsibility or the inner resources to tackle his illness.

Everything, as is the case with every alcoholic, has always been someone else's 19
fault, not his.

So we should not waste pity on Gascoigne, on the grounds that the man has prob- 20
ably manufactured enough of his own to last a lifetime. All alcoholics do. Is he any different from anyone with a serious drink problem and the classic pattern of behaviour — benders, appalling behaviour, violence; then, in the cold light of dawn, self-immolation, threats of suicide, pleas for forgiveness?

I hope psychiatric help and rehabilitation come to his aid. Like George Best, how- 21
ever, it may be that all Gascoigne wants to do is quietly continue his path of slow-motion self-destruction. If so, respect him, and respect his right to choose; but please do not sensationalise his illness.

Source: Melanie Reid © *The Times*/NI Syndication (25 February 2008)

Analysis questions

Identify and briefly explain the function of the following elements in the structure of this argument:

(a) 'We saw it with George Best...' (paragraph 2) (2 marks)

(b) 'There is sympathy. Of course there is.' (paragraph 6) (2 marks)

(c) 'Ah, Gazza's mad, that's the problem. He's had a breakdown. He's psychotic. It's his demons.' (paragraph 10) (2 marks)

(d) 'Research shows that 82 per cent of down-and-outs, of whatever age, have cognitive impairment from alcohol.' (paragraph 14) (2 marks)

■ ■ ■

A-grade answers

(a) George Best is used as an example of another celebrity footballer who was known for his drinking but is also widely admired.

(b) This is a response to an anticipated counter-argument that the author is being unsympathetic.

(c) This is a counter-argument that Gazza's behaviour is the result of mental illness rather than alcoholism.

(d) This is evidence used to support the argument that Gazza's mental problems are caused by his alcoholism.

e In each case, the candidate achieves both marks because the element is identified and its function briefly described.

■ ■ ■

C-grade answers

(a) An example

(b) A counter-argument

(c) A counter-argument

(d) Evidence

e In each case, the element is identified. In the answer to question (b), it would be more accurate to describe it as a response to a counter-argument.

These answers could expect to get 1 out of the 2 possible marks, for identifying the element. To achieve the second mark, the candidate needs to try to explain the function it performs.

When identifying an example, try to say what it is an example of.

When identifying evidence, try to say what it is evidence of.

Evaluation questions

Evaluate paragraphs 1–5. Assess the author's reasoning that women are right not to regard Gazza as a 'fallen titan'. (10 marks)

■ ■ ■

A-grade answer

Example: In the second paragraph, we have the example of George Best, so how useful is this example in supporting the author's argument? There are obvious parallels between Best and Gazza, both being great footballers who experienced alcohol problems in later life. The fact that 100,000 people turned out for Best's funeral indicates a great deal of public sympathy.

***Ad hominem*:** The author may be guilty of *ad hominem* (attacking the arguer rather than addressing the argument) in her reference to 'excitable male, middle-aged sports commentators'. It is unclear why their claims are weakened by their being male, middle-aged or excitable.

Restriction of the options: The author seems to present a false choice in suggesting that Gazza must be regarded either as a 'shattered genius' or as an alcoholic. This flaw weakens the argument because Gazza could be both a shattered genius and an alcoholic.

Generalisation: The main point in paragraphs 1–5 is that women hold the correct view in regarding Gazza as a simple alcoholic, seeing no tragedy in his situation. This would seem to be rather stereotypical and sexist, since it is unlikely that *all* men or *all* women would take the same view. The author is generalising, but does her argument rely on a sweeping generalisation that refuses to allow for exceptions?

Appeal to popularity: In claiming that women have a particular view of Gazza's situation, what point is the author seeking to make? One interpretation could be the author is arguing that, if women disagree with men, then women must be right. This would, of course, be straightforwardly sexist. Another interpretation could be that this is an appeal to popularity, with the author arguing that a great many people think something and therefore it must be true.

Overall, the author has asserted that women take a different view than men and this may enrage some readers who would feel that the author has been guilty of some sexist stereotyping. However, the key question is what is the *impact* of this argument? If it is true that women think one thing and men another, then so what? Even if women are in a numerical majority, does it necessarily follow that they must be right?

e This is an extremely detailed answer, considering the impact of a range of flaws.

■ ■ ■

question

C-grade answer

Para 1: 'Men become helplessly misty eyed' and 'women completely lose sympathy' are both statements stereotyping men and women, which does not necessarily represent them, so the usefulness is not of a very great extent. The phrase 'self-induced decline' immediately reminds the reader that Gazza's current state is his own fault.

Para 2: The example of George Best is used well to portray the fall of Paul Gascoigne, as both were successful players who later had alcohol problems.

Para 3: Illustrates how males 'interpret Gascoigne's fall as the latest episode of a Greek tragedy', which supports the author's reasoning, but it is flawed with inconsistency — she singles out Britain's 'excitable male, middle-aged sports commentators', which is *ad hominem* and then says 'for the rest of us' when before she was commenting on the difference of opinion of men compared to women.

Para 4: 'The female sex, which adores romance in all its forms', is a sweeping generalisation showing it is not a strong argument.

Para 5: Uses the word 'we' as if all women will agree with the author's opinion. Assuming it is the alcoholism that caused Gascoigne to go downhill, when it could be the mental illness that caused the alcoholism.

e It is true that the author was guilty of some outrageous stereotyping in saying that men think one thing and women another, but the candidate should pay more attention to the impact that this has on the reasoning. The key question is to what extent this stereotyping weakens the author's reasoning.

The candidate claims that there is some inconsistency in paragraph 3 but is unclear about what this inconsistency is supposed to be. The male, middle-aged sports commentators are men, so this reference is not inconsistent.

It is correct that the reference to the sports commentators being excitable and middle-aged is *ad hominem*, but the candidate should explain how and why this weakens the author's reasoning and what impact the flaw has.

The candidate does well to spot the possibility of reverse causation in noting that, while it is possible that alcoholism caused Gazza's decline, it is also possible that the decline caused the alcoholism. This perceptive point strengthens the candidate's response.

Question 3

Evaluate the author's reasoning in the remainder of her argument (paragraphs 6–21). How well does the reasoning support the main conclusion? (10 marks)

■ ■ ■

A-grade answer

Restriction of the options: The author's tendency to present her audience with a restriction of the options appears again in paragraphs 10 and 11. She suggests that some people (presumably the excitable, male middle-aged sports commentators) have focused on the fact that Gazza has been sectioned under the Mental Health Act and used this as a red herring to show that he is mentally ill rather than being an alcoholic. It is possible that Gazza is both mentally ill *and* an alcoholic but the author, once again, seems to present a false choice.

Straw man: This could also be seen as a straw man, since the sympathy of the sports commentators stems from the simple fact that Gazza has suffered a nervous breakdown, irrespective of what might have led to it.

Causation: Alternatively, this could be seen as reverse causation. The author says that Gazza's mental illness has been caused by his alcoholism but it could be the other way around — his alcoholism could have been caused by the mental illness.

Lack of relevant expertise: At the start of paragraph 12, the author confesses that she knows 'no more about Gascoigne's mental health than I read in the media'. This is a self-proclaimed lack of expertise, which could be said to weaken her reasoning. From her study of the tabloid press and without any apparent medical qualifications, the author has drawn the strong conclusion that Gazza's mental problems are probably the result of alcohol related brain damage (ARBD). This case is outlined at length in paragraphs 12–17.

Evidence: The reasoning in paragraphs 12–17 strengthens the author's argument because it clarifies the apparent restriction of the options in paragraphs 10 and 11. The author is accepting that Gazza has had a mental breakdown but she contends that this is not a sudden breakdown but one that has been caused by years of alcohol abuse. Her reasoning is strengthened by her use of relevant evidence but weakened because she has earlier confessed that she knows nothing more about this case than what she has read in the media.

Inconsistency: There is an apparent inconsistency at the start of paragraph 20, when the author says that 'we should not waste pity on Gascoigne'. This would appear to be inconsistent with statements elsewhere, such as in paragraph 6, where she says, 'There is sympathy. Of course there is.' Does the author feel sympathy or not? It is an important question because the author initially seemed to respond to an anticipated counter-argument that, whatever the reasons for his breakdown, Gazza is deserving of pity.

question

Conflation: A major weakness in this argument is conflation, which is where different words and terms are used interchangeably, even though they mean different things. In this argument, the author is objecting to the response, of some sections of the public, to Gazza's condition. In different parts of the argument she responds to:

- regarding Gazza as a shattered genius
- lionising Gazza
- regarding the situation as a tragedy/episode from a Greek tragedy
- regarding Gazza as heroic
- romanticising Gazza/seeing Gazza as a romantic figure
- sensationalising Gazza

These terms seem to be used interchangeably, yet they mean different things. By failing to clarify exactly what she is complaining about, the author is also at risk of attacking a straw man. The excitable, male middle-aged sports commentators certainly do regard Gazza as a shattered genius, at least insofar as great football skill can be regarded as genius, and that genius surely was shattered because Gazza's career was cut short and he has now suffered a breakdown. It is less easy to imagine why anyone would regard Gazza as a romantic figure. He may have been regarded as a hero at certain stages of his football career but it is unlikely that anyone would want to argue that the alleged assault on his wife and his sectioning under the Mental Health Act was 'heroic'. In distorting the views of those who sympathise with Gazza, the author has weakened her own argument.

e This is an extremely detailed evaluation of the argument, discussing the impact of a range of flaws in the reasoning.

■ ■ ■

C-grade answer

One of the main problems with the rest of the author's reasoning is that there are a number of inconsistencies with the author's reasoning. At first (paragraph 18) she states, 'I feel as sorry for him as I do for any damaged, addicted person'. She goes on to say that 'we should not waste pity on Gascoigne'. This contradicts her earlier argument and shows that her reasoning is not sound.

There is also a lack of expertise in her judgement of Gazza's condition. She states, 'I know no more about Gascoigne's health than I read in the media'. However, she then goes on to pass judgement about his condition, saying, 'I doubt that this is a story about sudden mental breakdown'. She has no more expertise than any member of the public and so she should not be evaluating his illness.

Her main reasoning does not support her conclusion that we should not 'sensationalise his illness', as most of the reasoning is flawed and does not always argue to support her conclusion.

e The first paragraph contains a good explanation of the inconsistency but its impact is not fully evaluated. The contradiction does weaken the argument but is the flaw fatal? The overall argument is not really about whether or not we should feel sympathy for Gazza but whether or not his illness should be sensationalised.

The second paragraph is a good explanation of the author's self-proclaimed lack of expertise, which weakens her reasoning about the cause of Gazza's condition.

Overall, this is a rather brief response. It contains two perceptive observations but more points of evaluation would be required to be eligible for the top mark bands. The candidate fails to adequately support the contention that 'most of the reasoning is flawed'.

Evaluate the effectiveness of the following counter-arguments in responding to the author's argument. (10 marks)

(a)

I am a woman, yet I feel desperately sorry for Paul Gascoigne. I resent the implication that I am somehow atypical of my gender or indeed that there should be a gender-typical response to such a situation.

I would also like to point out that, while ARBD is a common result of alcoholism, alcoholism is also a common result of mental health problems where the sufferer becomes locked into a spiral of self-medication. Not being privy to Paul's medical records, I would hesitate to make the confident diagnosis that Ms Reid seems to feel capable of.

Lucy Atkinson, Granville, France

(b)

Ms Reid, I'm afraid you've entirely missed the point. No one believes that Gascoigne was a 'genius' in any real sense of the word — quite the opposite, in almost every way imaginable. What *is* sad/tragic about his story is that he was ill-equipped to do much in life other than play football to wizardry standard, and when his short shelf-life was over his unremitting boozing seems to have filled the gap.

I don't know him personally and I never supported the teams he played for (except England) but I still feel very sad at the public and visible decline of someone who gave pleasure in his heyday to literally millions of people.

Unfortunately giving a lifetime's worth of wages in a year to young men sometimes has undesired (if predictable) effects, one of which is indulging to excess. The world is not perfect, so have some sympathy.

David, London, UK

■ ■ ■

A-grade answer

Generalisation: The first objection in Passage (a) is that Atkinson, as a woman, does sympathise with Gazza and she resents the assertion that she is atypical of her gender. The extent to which this counter-argument is effective depends on whether or not we can infer a sweeping generalisation in Melanie Reid's argument. If Reid means that *all* women share the same view, then the evidence of even a single woman who is atypical would be fatal to her claim. However, if this was a simple generalisation, then she is on safer ground. It may indeed be the case that Atkinson is atypical of her gender, no matter how much she may resent this being pointed out. Furthermore, Reid has not argued that women *should* share this gender-typical response.

Causation/expertise: Second, Atkinson raises the possibility of reverse causation. It could be, as Reid argues, that Gazza's mental problems were caused by alcoholism but it could also be the case that his alcoholism was caused by pre-existing mental problems. This reasoning does weaken a large part of Reid's argument (particularly her reasoning in paragraphs 10–17). If it is true that there is a possibility of reverse causation, it is reasonable of Atkinson to claim that access to Gazza's medical records would be necessary to make a diagnosis and this further weakens Reid's argument, since she does make a confident diagnosis, despite admitting that she knows no more about Gazza's case than what she has read in the media.

Straw man: Passage (b) addresses effectively the problem that Reid fails to adequately define terms such as 'genius' or 'tragic'. It is effective in countering Reid's argument because it identifies the straw man of suggesting that anyone would regard Gazza's off-the-field activities as genius.

Causation: Passage (b) is also effective in countering the author's argument in identifying yet another potential cause of the breakdown. It is possible that Gazza's alcoholism *and* subsequent breakdown were caused by a third factor, which could be the pressures associated with attention, money and celebrity experienced by Gazza when he suddenly came to prominence as a result of his footballing talent.

Inconsistency: Passage (b) also suggests that the public should feel sad for Gazza. At several points in her argument, Reid seems to anticipate this counterclaim by emphasising that she is sympathetic, on a human level, for Gazza as she would be for any ill person. However, as previously explained, she is not entirely consistent and she may have revealed her true feelings in paragraph 20 when she argues that 'we should not waste pity on Gascoigne'.

This is a thorough response. Several relevant points of evaluation have been made and the candidate has considered the extent to which the original author's argument is damaged.

■ ■ ■

C-grade answer

Passage (a)

This is a good counter-argument as for one it proves how it is not only men who feel sorry for Gazza, which proves she was generalising.

It also shows how her lack of expertise has led to the condition ARBD not being fully researched by the author, as it can create addiction as well as coming as a result of it.

Passage (b)

This is a good counter-argument as it attacks her straw man argument where she had changed the argument to focus on his own faults. Here the writer looks at the outside influences that have led to his slow decline. For example, he mentions the

high wage he was paid and the lack of support he received once his 'shelf life' had ended.

e In the first paragraph, the candidate's understanding of what is meant by 'generalising' is fairly unsophisticated. The author of the original article is certainly guilty of stereotyping, but the evidence of a single female who fails to conform to this stereotype does not do great damage to the overall argument.

The second paragraph is quite sound, as far as it goes. The response could be strengthened if the candidate were to explore to what extent this lack of expertise weakens the original author's argument.

The third paragraph is stronger, especially as the candidate picks up on the element of 'straw man' in the original argument to show that Reid does not really understand what she is attacking.

Arguments

'Celebrities are as entitled to their privacy as anyone else.' Write your own argument to challenge or support this claim. (20 marks)

DEFINITIONS: At the start of the argument, it is important to define key words. In this argument, the words 'privacy', 'celebrities' and 'entitled' could be usefully defined:

- Privacy could mean the freedom from public attention. You would need to think about what this can mean in practice. It could mean the freedom of the individual from the attention of the government or other authorities such as the police or employers. It can also relate to the freedom from the intrusion of the media.
- A celebrity would usually be regarded as anyone who is, for whatever reason, famous and in the public eye. This can include a wide range of people, from those who have deliberately sought fame to others who have not sought to be famous.
- An entitlement means a 'right'. This would normally mean that there is some law that protects this right and some obligation on the part of others. If I have a right to privacy, then this means that others have an obligation to respect my privacy.

In framing the parameters of the question, it is also important to distinguish between *is* and *ought*. Is this a moral question or simply a legal question? If you have studied A-level law, you might be aware of what the law *is* on this issue; otherwise, you would probably write about what the law *ought* to be and what rights people *should* have.

PRINCIPLES: Be careful not to confuse Units F503 and F504. The F504 argument does not have to use ethical principles to resolve a dilemma. However, where dilemmas arise and where principles might be useful in resolving those dilemmas, this could be explored. When the issue of privacy is debated, principles are often proposed. For example, the assertion that there is a 'right to privacy' is a general principle, which often comes into conflict with the principle of 'the freedom of the press'.

Dilemmas can arise. If we protect the right to privacy, it could mean that the public will be prevented from obtaining important information about public figures, but if the press has absolute freedom, individuals could suffer unwarranted intrusion into their private lives.

Maybe you can seek to resolve this dilemma in your argument. It is often suggested that there should be a distinction between celebrities who are figures of national importance, such as politicians or judges, and other 'celebrities' such as footballers or musicians. If politicians seek public office and exercise power over the lives of ordinary people, perhaps they should expect public scrutiny of

their private lives. The press can be seen as the 'watchdog' of democracy, ensuring that public figures are held to account in the 'public interest'.

The phrase 'public interest' itself requires definition. Just because the public is interested in something, it does not follow that the matter is in the public interest.

It would also be useful to define what we mean by a 'public figure'. Politicians and judges clearly are public figures in positions of authority but, in other cases, the distinction is less clear. What about civil servants or chief executives or police officers or teachers? Should the private lives of these professionals be exposed to public scrutiny?

HYPOCRISY: Those who argue for press freedom often point out that some politicians use their families for political purposes, for example by printing their photographs on their election leaflets. In the past, some politicians have campaigned on 'family values' or 'public decency' issues and have then been found to be leading less than wholesome lives themselves after the revelation of scandals in their private lives. If a politician, for example, campaigns against drug use and is then found to be a drug user, is this not an aspect of that person's private life that should be made public?

Another issue of alleged hypocrisy relates to some celebrities who seek to put themselves in the public eye but then complain about media intrusion. They may, for example, take money from a celebrity magazine for 'exclusive' photographs of their home, their new baby or their wedding and then complain when the paparazzi photograph them in the street. Should celebrities, who make their living out of media attention, inviting and encouraging public interest into their private lives, really be able to exercise total control over what gets printed and what does not?

EXAMPLES: You should be able to think of some relevant examples of media intrusion into the private lives of celebrities. Here are three suggestions:

- Max Mosley is the president of the FIA, which governs Formula One motorsport. He also happens to be the son of the much reviled Sir Oswald Mosley, who was the leader of the British Union of Fascists in the 1930s. Max Mosley successfully won a legal case for invasion of privacy against a national newspaper that had printed photographs of him engaged in a sadomasochistic orgy with five prostitutes. Does being leader of the FIA make Mosley a public figure? Is the identity of his father in any way relevant to this case? Is his sex life a matter of public interest?
- Princess Diana was continually hounded by the press and many people alleged that paparazzi photographers were at least partly to blame for her death. Princess Diana was clearly a public figure, being the ex-wife of the Prince of Wales and mother of the future king. During her life, the press often claimed that Diana was hypocritical in inviting public attention on some occasions and then objecting to it at other times.

- Former prime minister Tony Blair and his wife Cherie often paraded their children for photographs on political occasions but they complained about the media attention given to their 16-year-old son Euan when he was picked up by the police for being so drunk that he was unable to walk after a night spent celebrating his GCSE results. Euan Blair gave the police a false name, an old address and a date of birth that would have made him 18 (the legal age to buy alcohol). Tony Blair had recently introduced new measures to crack down on young offenders.

CONCLUSION: The conclusion should be either that celebrities *are* as entitled to their privacy as everyone else or that they *are not*.

It is important to establish to what extent ordinary people are entitled to privacy, in order to argue whether or not celebrities should be held to the same standard.

There are some strong arguments on both sides but you should not feel a need to 'sit on the fence' — the question asks you to argue for or against the claim. This does not mean that you have to take an extreme position. You could argue that there is an absolute right to privacy or that the freedom of the press should be absolute; alternatively, you could take a more moderate position that there should be checks and balances.

■ ■ ■

Sample arguments

Candidate A

Celebrity can be defined as a person or group of people who are well known and information, pictures and stories about them are printed or presented in the media. Privacy can be defined, for the purposes of this argument, as the concealment of information, pictures and stories by a person's choice.

In today's society, which seems to be driven mainly by gossip and scandal, celebrities are the prime target of the media. Celebrities have risen to fame and are part of the pop-culture of the world we live in. It can be argued that the media have an intent and even a right to intrude on celebrities and report on their activities. This is a repercussion of celebrity. Some would argue that these people should have a right to privacy but surely to gain fame you have to be a public figure and therefore have to sacrifice this privacy in order to 'become public'.

It has been said that, in order to maintain their status, celebrities 'tip off' the media of their location in order to arrange a rendezvous and thus create an 'accidental' photo opportunity. A recent study suggested that this was on the rise as faded celebs try to regain some of the limelight. This therefore means that celebrities want their lives to be exposed, albeit on their terms.

It can otherwise be argued that celebrities want their lives to be kept private, such as the case of author J. K. Rowling, who recently sued the *Daily Mirror* for printing a

photo of her daughter Jessica. But this is the only case in recent years of this type and it also involves a minor which means that different rules apply, thus making this example non-applicable to a modern celebrity.

A buzz world of the current government is 'transparency', i.e. demonstrating every step of a process to show that nothing untoward is occurring. Our MPs are elected by the public to represent us and thus we have the right to know exactly what our elected figures are doing, saying and not saying. It can be argued that celebrities are the same. Although they are not elected, it is still by a public process that they are famous. If it weren't for the public appreciation, they would not be a celebrity. Thus we have the right to know of what they are doing with the wealth they have as a result of the public.

Therefore celebrities should accept that a lack of privacy and a life in the public eye is all part of the package and thus can't be protected by law.

e The argument starts well with a definition of the words 'privacy' and 'celebrity'.

The second paragraph contains a simple counterclaim, that celebrities 'have a right to privacy', which is adequately dismissed by the reasoning elsewhere in the paragraph. This counterclaim could be developed into a more sophisticated counter-argument.

The third paragraph contains a clear reason, some supporting evidence and an intermediate conclusion in the last sentence.

The fourth paragraph starts with a counter-argument that uses an example (J. K. Rowling) as support. The candidate attempts to dismiss this counter-argument by questioning the relevance of the example. The candidate does not dismiss the counter-argument very convincingly because many other celebrities have children and so it is difficult to see why the example is 'non-applicable to a modern celebrity'.

The fifth paragraph has a developed reason, based on a principle, leading to an intermediate conclusion that we have a right to know what celebrities are doing.

The argument ends with a clear statement of a conclusion.

Overall, despite the problems with the fourth paragraph, this is a strong response. The argument is well structured with clear strands of reasoning, intermediate conclusions, definition, examples and evidence. The argument is generally consistent and persuasive.

This answer would be awarded a Grade A/B.

Candidate B

In my opinion, everyone, including celebrities, is entitled to their privacy being protected by law. For the purposes of this argument, I will say that a celebrity is someone in the public eye who is known and recognisable by members of the public.

Privacy can be defined as keeping the personal aspects of a person's life to themselves. I believe that everybody has the right to have their privacy protected.

When we read newspapers and magazines, the people that we see continuously featured are the people who want their lives in view. Celebrities like Kerry Katona and Victoria Beckham like to be in the limelight and so they invite media attention. These people have the right to their own privacy but prefer to lead public lives by appearing on reality television shows, creating their own television programmes or inviting magazines to come to their homes to take photos of them and then write an article about how beautiful their house is.

We do not live in a 'nanny state' but if there is information that is needed for our protection by the government then this is acceptable and not an invasion of privacy. It is only an invasion of our privacy when it is splashed on the front page of various tabloid newspapers. Therefore everyone has the right to have their private life kept private from the general public.

I do not think that someone's private life affects their ability to do their job. If a politician is found to have used a prostitute, it is none of our business or concern. It is only our concern if their private life is having a negative effect on their ability to do their job.

It could be argued that some celebrities get unwanted attention from the media but it is up to individuals whether they want to talk about their private lives openly or to keep this information to themselves. If harassment continues, there is always the possibility of taking out a restraining order against paparazzi, which is where the law comes into the equation. For these celebrities who are only famous for being in the news, this is not an option.

Even though everyone has the right to have their privacy protected by law, some people do not want this and so they choose to keep their private lives very much public.

e The argument starts well with a definition of the words 'privacy' and 'celebrity'. The main conclusion, that everyone has the right to have their privacy protected, is also to be found in the first paragraph.

There are some examples in the second paragraph of celebrities who choose to live their lives in the public eye but it is not entirely clear what the relevance of these examples is. This paragraph would benefit from an intermediate conclusion to show what the candidate is concluding from the reasoning. Without any intermediate conclusion, the reasoning would seem to be either inconsistent or irrelevant because no one is suggesting that celebrities should not be allowed to be celebrities. The candidate would do better to explore the counter-argument that, by voluntarily choosing to invite the media into their lives, some celebrities should accept that they will sometimes be subject to unwanted intrusion.

The third paragraph does finish with an intermediate conclusion, that everyone has the right to have their private life kept private. However, this intermediate conclusion

question

is not well supported by the preceding reasoning. The candidate fails to offer a strong reason to support the intermediate conclusion.

The fourth paragraph seems to address the counter-argument that there is an important social need for people to know what public figures, such as politicians, are up to. The candidate responds to this view but the reasoning is somewhat inconsistent with the main conclusion because the candidate seems to accept that some public figures should be subject to some intrusion, where what they are doing affects their ability to do their jobs.

The fifth paragraph starts with a counterclaim, which the candidate then responds to. There is a good reason in this paragraph, which is that some people cannot afford to use the courts to protect their privacy. Again, the reasoning would benefit from an intermediate conclusion to move the argument forward. If the current legal options are inadequate, what extension does the candidate suggest?

The final paragraph seems to be a repetition of the reasoning in paragraph 2, that some celebrities welcome media attention. Does this mean that such celebrities should not be able to keep any aspect of their lives private?

Although there are some good elements in this argument, such as definition, examples and use of counter-argument, the reasoning to support the main conclusion is fairly weak. The argument could be strengthened with a more disciplined use of intermediate conclusions.

This answer would be awarded a Grade C/D.

Candidate C

First of all, should members of the general public have their privacy protected by law? On the other hand, it is a long kept principle by all human societies that people should be entitled to have a private life, mostly because most people have some form of secret or skeleton in their closet that they don't want to share with the rest of the world and we are alright with this because most of us have secrets of our own and if we made others divulge theirs we would have to divulge the facts of our own lives. Also we often view it as harmless because most people's secrets are not of any relevance or danger to us.

On the other hand, we should be entitled to know if our next-door neighbours' secrets happen to be that they are serial killers or convicted sex offenders. Thus we have come to a balance in our society that you are perfectly entitled to a private life provided you do not do anything illegal.

Then there is the issue of whether or not celebrities should be included in this. Celebrities often argue that we the general public are entitled to private lives, so why shouldn't they be? However, the counter-argument is that celebrities have made ridiculous amounts of money and a career out of being in the public eye and so they have already made the choice to exchange their privacy for money and fame.

I think we have come to a balance with most of society and should come to a balance with celebrities as well. The argument that they have made the decision to trade privacy for fame and money has validity but that shouldn't be used to exonerate the paparazzi or the obsessive stalkers that many celebrities are subjected to.

This argument does not have a clear conclusion. The candidate's view seems to be that we should strive for 'a balance' but there is no real explanation of what this balance should be in practice. Overall, the candidate tends to want to 'sit on the fence' rather than arguing a way towards a clear conclusion.

To understand the argument, we have to understand that the candidate is arguing for balance. There are a couple of strands of reasoning in which there is an attempt to show that there is merit in both sides of the debate.

There is some inconsistency. For example, the candidate establishes a principle in the second paragraph that 'you are perfectly entitled to a private life provided you do not do anything illegal'. However, the candidate then abandons this principle by arguing that celebrities have 'made the choice to exchange their privacy for money and fame'.

There are no examples or intermediate conclusions. The candidate does not define any key terms.

Overall, this is a very weak response that may just reach grade E.